MARRIED SAINTS

MARRIED SAINTS

BY

SELDEN P. DELANY

The Newman Press
Westminster, Maryland

1950

𝔑𝔦𝔥𝔦𝔩 𝔒𝔟𝔰𝔱𝔞𝔱: Arthur J. Scanlan, S.T.D., *Censor Librorum*
𝔍𝔪𝔭𝔯𝔦𝔪𝔞𝔱𝔲𝔯: ✠ Patrick Cardinal Hayes, *Archbishop*, New York

New York, July 29, 1935

278.227
D37m
1950

First Printing, 1935
Reprinted, 1950

Manufactured by
Universal Lithographers, Inc.
Baltimore 2, Md.
U. S. A.

PREFACE

MANY people hold that sanctity is incompatible with marriage. The purpose of this book is to illustrate that sanctity may be attained in the marriage state as well as in a life of celibacy ; for a saint is one who tries in all things to conform himself to the will of God. Or, as Mr. Chesterton once said, "A saint is a man who is very much like the rest of us — only very different."

Now, there are two kinds of saints — they may be designated as common and heroic. An immense number of Catholics who are living good lives in a state of grace have attained to a state of common sanctity. Heroic saints are those who have developed either the theological virtues of faith, hope and charity, or the cardinal virtues of justice, prudence, temperance and fortitude to an heroic degree. It is saints of this kind that are canonized by the Church.

Lest some diligent readers observe that in this book I have included several biographies of men and women who are not enrolled in the Roman Catholic calendar of saints, I wish to explain that those men

[v]

and women were eminent for piety and virtue, and that in the final decision regarding their sanctity I submit to the judgment of the Church. In most cases, however, steps have already been taken to introduce their causes in Rome.

THIS book had its origin in a talk with one of my friends at the Beda College in Rome, Father Anthony Thorold. We were discussing the nature of sanctity, and I felt that he overemphasized the qualities of austerity, and was a little inclined to regard sanctity as impossible outside the religious life. This is only natural in one who had spent six years in a Carthusian monastery and had relinquished his aim only because of a break-down in health. In contending for the possibility of sanctity in every walk of life, I said laughingly that I would like to write a book sometime on "Married Saints."

The next morning, Father Thorold surprised me by saying that he had been thinking over what I had said, and that he thought it would be an excellent idea to bring out a book on Married Saints. This encouragement from one whose judgment I valued so highly prompted me to take up the subject in earnest. I worked on it during my next three summer vacations, which were spent in England, gathering most of my material in the British Museum.

Subsequently, I decided to give up the idea of publishing the book. The reasons were : first, that I had discovered that I had no great gifts for writing biographical sketches of this sort ; secondly, that I did not feel that I had the knowledge of paleography which it seemed to me was required to make such a study thoroughly ; thirdly, I had come to feel that some of the men and women of whom I had written had not become saints until they had ceased to be married. I would have felt more comfortable if in recent times the Church had canonized some man or woman who was married.

The canonization of Saint Thomas More reassured me and revived the idea of submitting my manuscript to a publisher. Almost at the same time Miss Julie Kernan of Longmans, Green and Company, to whom I had confided in an unguarded moment some three years before in Paris that I was working on such a book, came to me and asked if I had finished the book and whether I would not submit the manuscript to Longmans for examination. I did so, and after examining the manuscript they decided upon its publication.

SELDEN P. DELANY

New York
July 1, 1935

[vii]

CONTENTS

	PAGE
SANCTITY AND MARRIAGE	1
MARRIAGE IN PAGANISM AND CHRISTIANITY	13
SOME PRACTICAL ASPECTS OF MYSTICAL EXPERIENCE	26
SAINT MONICA [331-387]	40
SAINT PAULINUS OF NOLA [353-431]	57
SAINT MARGARET OF SCOTLAND [1045-1083]	76
SAINT ELIZABETH OF HUNGARY [1207-1231]	91
SAINT LOUIS OF FRANCE [1214-1270]	110
SAINT FRANCES OF ROME [1384-1440]	129
BLESSED NICHOLAS OF FLÜE (1417-1487)	152
SAINT THOMAS MORE [1478-1535]	173
MADAME ACARIE [1566-1618]	192
BLESSED ANNA MARIA TAIGI [1769-1837]	211
MOTHER ELIZABETH SETON [1774-1821]	224
THE MARRIED LIFE OF CORNELIA CONNELLY [1809-1879]	246

MARRIED SAINTS

PAGE

Louis Veuillot [1813-1883] 254

Frederic Ozanam [1813-1853] 269

Elizabeth Arrighi Leseur [1866-1914] . 291

Lucie Félix-Faure Goyau [1866-1913] . 299

Three Apostles of Catholic Action . . 312

   Giambattista Paganuzzi [1830-1910] . . 316

   Giuseppe Toniolo [1845-1918] . . . 321

   Ludovico Necchi [1876-1930] . . . 329

MARRIED SAINTS

SANCTITY AND MARRIAGE

I

THE canonization of Blessed Thomas More was extremely significant for many reasons : he was an Englishman, a layman, a man of great learning, a humanist, and he died as a martyr to his belief in papal supremacy. More than any other man, perhaps, he was the typical Englishman. His humor, versatility, and literary achievements have endeared him to multitudes of persons in every part of the English-speaking world. His canonization is notable also for the fact that he was a married man — indeed twice married. It is a long time since any married saint has been officially canonized by the Catholic Church. That so few married people have been raised to the Church's altars since the present process of canonization was initiated, raises the query whether sanctity is necessarily incompatible with married life.

To answer this question we must first clarify our minds as to what are the constituent elements of sanctity. Many think that a saint is simply one who lives according to high moral standards. But one can live such a life without any conscious relationship with God. A saint is one whose whole life is motivated by the love of God, and who tries daily to do the will of God, as that will is made known to him through vocation and circumstances. According to the degree of sanctity, saints are divided into common and heroic saints.

For obvious reasons it is only the heroic saints that are canonized by the Church. Before any servant of God can be enrolled in the canon of the saints it must be established beyond peradventure that his or her life was distinguished by the heroic practice of faith, hope, charity, justice, temperance, fortitude and prudence. That is the norm according to which the Sacred Congregation judges in the process of canonization.

In the cloistered life heroic love of God may be manifested in self-abnegation, continence, the cheerful acceptance of poverty and suffering, prayer and obedience. In married life it shines forth in patient endurance, mutual forbearance, sacrifices for the children, mutual faithfulness and affection, control of the sex instinct, and extraordinary self-denial. Under both sets of circumstances saints are developed — whether in the same proportion God only knows. Not even all heroic saints have been formally canonized by the Church. Religious orders are more likely to take the necessary steps towards the canonization of one of their members than a private family, especially if the living members of the family are either worldly or poor, or if they think that the saint was too generous in distributing the family inheritance.

Unusual mystical experiences, such as visions, ecstatic prayer, or the awareness of the divine action in the soul, are not essential to establish the heroic sanctity that is required for canonization. They are given at God's pleasure and possibly may be conditioned in some way by natural character and temperament.

The Catholic Church asserts the rights of all her children to sanctity. This teaching of the Church found special expression in Saint Francis de Sales, who delighted in leading men and women of the world into the sanctuary of perfection. He taught that one could live the saintly life anywhere — in the army, the court, the university, the world of commerce or the home.

Retirement from the world, though good both for the souls who are called by God to leave the world, and for the world which they help to sanctify by their prayers and vicarious sufferings, is not the only road to sanctity. In this and every age, there has always been an urgent need for saints who are in the world but not of it, engaged in secular work, and committed to the ordinary human relationships — family life, business activities, politics, art, science, literature. There is no reason why we should not have such saints.

Such an outpouring of divine grace would make Christian standards of living more familiar to the indifferent and worldly, hasten the return of the world to a Catholic culture, and diffuse more widely the contagion of Catholic sanctity. Cloistered souls are far removed from the daily trials and temptations of their brethren living in the world. They have taken up their abode in the land of far distances, in peaceful valleys amid majestic mountain peaks ; but the friends they have left behind sometimes feel that they have been deserted. However, those who have renounced the world have obeyed the call of God, and God's wisdom may not be questioned.

II

Is sanctity then incompatible with marriage ? Not a few would hold that it is, and perhaps on a superficial view of the facts a plausible argument might be constructed. Saint Paul went so far as to say "He that is without a wife is solicitous for the things that belong to the Lord : how he may please God. But he that is with a wife is solicitous for the things of the world ; how he may please his wife." That might suggest the inference that, in the opinion of Saint Paul, a married man could not be a saint.

Most of the saints commemorated in the Church's calendar have been bishops, priests or religious. Many of the canonized married saints were either martyrs, or royal saints who married for reasons of state or who separated by mutual consent and became religious, or when the husband or wife died the other embraced the monastic life. It must be admitted that few married women, whose husbands have outlived them, have been canonized. There have been many saintly widows, but a husband in the flesh seems to be an obstacle to sanctity. Wives have not so often been obstacles to the sanctification of their husbands. Nevertheless it is noteworthy that while the number of saints who have been beatified or canonized in the last four centuries has been between four and five hundred, of these more than three hundred belonged to religious orders. From this it might be inferred, that both the Church and the saints have been lukewarm in their devotion to the married state.

In reply to this argument we may say that it is quite to be expected that the religious life should prove to be pre-eminently the school for sanctity. Moreover, a sufficient proof that marriage and sanctity are not mutually contradictory is to be found in the actual practice of the Church in canonizing many men and women who were married.

In Our Lord's teaching both marriage and celibacy are approved. After He had laid down the principle of the indissolubility of marriage, His disciples concluded that it might be better not to marry. "If the case of a man with his wife be so, it is expedient not to marry." [1] In His reply He emphasized two points. First, He re-affirmed His previous declaration that the marriage bond may not be dissolved. Secondly, He explained that celibacy, when chosen for supernatural motives with a view to the heavenly life, is praiseworthy. This state of life, however, is only for those who have been favored with a special grace of illumination and fortitude. "He that can receive it, let him receive it." Every one is free either to marry or not to marry. The choice of the single state must be free from constraint. There are three classes of celibates in the world: those who are naturally inclined to continence; those who are violently compelled to live a single life; and those who voluntarily adopt celibacy "for the

[1] Matthew xxix, 10.

sake of the kingdom of Heaven"—that is to be more free to serve the Church.[1]

Thus Our Lord both restored marriage to its pristine purity, and made celibacy and virginity a matter of vocation. Just because He sanctified marriage, rendered it indissoluble, and made it a sacrament of His Church, He thereby gave His divine sanction to the life of continence and chastity. There will always be those who feel that they cannot submit to the indissoluble bond of marriage, but wish to preserve their individual liberty of action. With all their hearts they aspire to the ideal and heavenly life, and desire to be free to make as generous an offering of themselves as possible to the service of God.

Saint Paul settled the question of the relative good of continence and marriage in these words: "I would that all men were even as myself. But every man hath his proper gift from God: one after this manner and another after that."[2] Sanctity, therefore may be attained in either state.

The conclusion, therefore, to which we are led is that both celibacy and marriage are in accordance with the will of God, and that it is entirely a matter

[1] *Méditations sur la vie de Notre Seigneur Jésus Christ*, by P. M. Meschler, S. J., vol. II, p. 369.
[2] 1 Corinthians vii, 7.

of vocation which state anyone shall enter. That being so, it is abundantly clear that one may attain to sanctity either in the single life or in the married life.

The reason why so few married saints have been canonized is probably to be found in the fact that the marriage state from its very nature does not provide such a favorable ground as the unmarried state for heroic sanctity on the grand scale — that is for such a complete holocaust of one's life as to make it possible for the heroism involved to attract the notice of onlookers. It will be only in such latter cases as a rule that sufficient evidence of heroicity could be available. Just as the military authorities in a war can only single out for the award of an honorable medal those cases of courage which were readily observable, so the Church can apply her formal process of canonization only on similar principles.

III

To assert that men and women may become saints in the married state, if marriage is their vocation, is not to assert that there is no difference in merit — that is in the rewards they will receive in heaven — between those who follow the evangelical counsels of poverty, chastity and obedience, and those who live merely according to the commandments. It can hardly be denied that those who forsake all to follow Christ will lay up greater treasure in heaven than those who direct their own affairs in the midst of possessions and family life, even though their wills be perfectly conformed to the will of God.

That the life of the counsels is considered by the Church to be on a higher plane than the life of the precepts is clear from the declaration of the Council of Trent : "If anyone shall say that the married state is to be placed above the state of virginity or celibacy, and that it is not better and more blessed to remain in virginity or celibacy than to be joined in marriage, let him be anathema."

Every one is free to choose between the married state and celibacy, but he cannot attain to sanctity unless he makes his choice in the light of divine vocation. The choice may be determined by personal taste, capacity, natural inclination, temperament and so forth. Before coming to a decision, it is well that one should seriously count the cost of either course.

Whether people marry or remain single, sanctity is out of the question for them unless they are obedient to the call of God. This point has been well brought out by Father Bede Jarrett :

MARRIED SAINTS

There are souls that can only develop the gifts within them through the married life. Their souls left solitary would be maimed, never achieving their real richness. There are others whom God has designed for the way of the cloister — separate, untouched, alone. Each has to find the place to which God calls him and for which he was destined and endowed. His vocation is a positive way of life. The married life, if it is God's choice for you, will contain for you the highest thing you can ever do. One way of life may be higher than another way of life, one way of prayer higher than another, but this can only be in the abstract, for that is highest for me which God has called me to — whatever it may be. To do God's will is the noblest thing ; by this only are both cloister and the way of marriage justified.[1]

Those who would like to marry, and feel that it is their vocation, but are denied the means or the opportunity — and there is an increasing number of such in the modern world — must learn to convert the sex instinct into energizing forces in their work, and in the human relationship which God brings to them. An involuntary celibacy is their vocation, and it is often a more difficult one than marriage or the religious life, just because it is so contrary to their desires. These people are deserving of our utmost forbearance and sympathy. In the Middle Ages, when life was more simple, people either married or went into the priesthood or a religious order.

[1] *House of Gold*, New York, 1931, p. 95.

Our modern industrial civilization, the high cost of living, and the economic independence of women have changed all that. These involuntary celibates — both men and women — who must live in the world, have a real opportunity of becoming saints.

In these days, when so many look upon marriage as a union of pleasure or self-interest, a step towards money and position, or merely as a means of perpetuating the race, there is need for insistence on the fact that Christian marriage is the union before God of two souls who wish, by the grace of the sacrament to perfect one another, to love one another, and to give children to the Church and saints to heaven.

This higher aim has been stressed by His Holiness Pius XI in the Encyclical *Casti Connubii :* "The love then of which we are speaking is not based on the passing lust of the moment nor does it consist in pleasing words only, but in the deep attachment of the heart which is expressed in action, since love is proved by deeds. This outward expression of love in the home demands not only mutual help but must go further ; must have as its primary purpose that man and wife help each other day by day in forming and perfecting themselves in the interior life, so that through their partnership in life they may advance ever more and more in virtue, and above all that they may grow in true love towards God and their neighbor, on which indeed 'dependeth the whole Law of the Prophets.' For all men of every condition, in whatever honorable walk of life they may be, can and ought to imitate that most perfect example of holiness placed before man by God, namely Christ Our Lord, and by God's grace to arrive at the summit of perfection, as is proved by the examples of many saints."

MARRIAGE IN PAGANISM AND
CHRISTIANITY

I

In the early years of the Roman republic, paganism was a fairly wholesome religion which inculcated the natural virtues that enabled Rome to conquer the world : a sound family life, a love of liberty, a religious reverence for the right, a respect for a man's sworn faith, exact obedience to the laws even when cruel, and a stern avoidance of luxury. Roman men were frugal, austere and hard-working ; and divided their time between agriculture and war. They held their wives in high respect and jealously guarded their daughters from evil.

After 150 B.C. degeneration set in, luxury and debauchery abounded, marriage was despised, bachelors became numerous, children were slain and exposed until laws had to be passed requiring people to bring up the children to whom they gave birth. Divorce soon became widely prevalent ; the degradation of the Roman matrons was so notorious that Seneca, the contemporary of Saint Paul, exclaimed, "Women are ignorant, unruly creatures, incapable of governing themselves."

So greatly had family life declined by the time of Augustus that a law was introduced which gave valuable advantages to every citizen who had as many as three children : an unrestricted right to receive bequests, a double share in the public distributions of food or money, exemption from numerous public duties, speedier promotion to honors and a seat in the best part of the theatre. This law, however, was rendered useless by a provision which exempted from its operation vestal virgins, soldiers and bachelors. The family continued to decay.

Tacitus in his *De Moribus Germanorum* obliquely hinted at the deterioration of Roman women by emphasizing the higher moral standards of the women of Germania : "They are preserved by the safeguards of innocence, remote from the spectacles which contaminate, and far from the festivals which kindle passions. . . In this land they do not laugh at vices. To corrupt and to yield to corruption is not called 'living up to one's century. . .' To limit the number of their children or to kill one of the new-born is held to be a crime." [1]

Another sign of degradation in Roman family life was the change in the method of educating girls.

[1] Chapter XIX.

They were no longer kept secluded from early childhood in the homes of their parents. It was considered old-fashioned for them to grow up under
their mother's eyes, to learn to spin and weave and
to train themselves for the duties of married life.
Their education was largely handed over to Greek
slaves. Co-education also became common.

Scipio Emilianus wrote : "When I entered one of
those schools to which nobles send their sons, I found
more than five hundred young girls and boys, who,
in the company of players and infamous characters,
were taking lessons on the lyre, or in singing and
deportment. I saw one child twelve years old, the
son of a candidate, executing a dance unworthy of
the lewdest servant."[1]

However we may account for it, we may not dispute the historical fact that in the classical culture of
the Mediterranean world the patriarchal family was
dying out and the citizen class becoming sterile, when
Christianity began to lift its head as a force to be
reckoned with.

Mr. Christopher Dawson has thus described the
situation : "Conditions of life both in the Greek City
State and in the Roman Empire favored the man
without a family who could devote his whole ener-
gies to the duties and pleasures of public life. Late

[1] Macrobius, *Saturnalia*, II, 10.

marriages and small families became the rule and men satisfied their sexual instinct by homo-sexuality or by relations with slaves and prostitutes. This aversion to marriage and the deliberate restriction of the family by the practice of infanticide and abortion was undoubtedly the main cause of the decline of ancient Greece, as Polybius pointed out in the second century B.C." [1]

Polybius wrote that in his days the diminution of population in Greece was so great that towns were becoming deserted and the fields untilled. The reason for this was neither war nor pestilence, but that men "owing to vanity, avarice or cowardice, no longer wished to marry or to bring up children."

In the early days of the Empire, Roman women were becoming emancipated. Intoxicated by their new freedom they tried to rule over men. Realizing that they were mistresses of their own persons and others' as well, they grew more violent, haughty and unbearable. They wielded their domestic authority with pitiless severity, tormenting their husbands and beating their slaves. The women of the decadent Roman Empire also began to take up occupations and trades that had formerly been reserved to men. Women advocates and law-makers

[1] Christopher Dawson, *Christianity and Sex*, Criterion Miscellany No. 13, p. 22.

became numerous and there were even feminine athletes and gladiators. In the words of a contemporary satirist, "they fled their sex." [1]

Men renounced fatherhood to devote themselves to base pleasures. As the number of childless women increased they lapsed more frequently into immorality. Greater facilities for divorce rendered marriage little better than legalized prostitution. These disorders enervated and corrupted the upper classes and from them spread to the proletarian masses who degenerated into a servile horde, listless and lazy, whose one cry was "give us bread and games !"

II

CHRISTIANITY re-established the family on a more enduring basis and amid the ruins of the declining civilization of Rome laid the foundations of a new European social order. The Christian family, though it embodied the old patriarchal tradition that had prevailed among the Jews and the ruling classes of Greece and Rome, was in certain notable respects a new institution. It made the wife the equal of the husband, because according to Christian teaching he belonged to her exclusively and they had mutual obligations toward each other. It was open to every

[1] Bossier, *La Religion Romaine*, vol. II, p. 232.

class, even to slaves. Most important of all, marriage was elevated into a sacrament which by its qualities of love, faithfulness and indissolubility, symbolized the union of Christ with His Church.

In proportion as the Roman Empire declined in vital energy, the Catholic Church became more vigorous and influential. One of the chief reasons for the rapid growth of the Church was that her standards of family life were higher than those of the pagan civilization around her. Christian men and women were not afraid to have children. While the pagan population declined from divorce and birth control, the ranks of the Christians multiplied not only because of a higher birth-rate, but also because of the steadily increasing number of conversions.

Why was it that gifted Greek and Roman philosophers, like Zeno, Epicurus, Epictetus and Seneca, even when backed up by rich men and statesmen who controlled legislation and the public expenditures could not devise anything like the Church's agencies for the care of the poor, the sick and the orphans, to say nothing of creating an enduring family life? The explanation is to be found in the complete dissimilarity in their first principles. Pagan philosophers regarded philanthropy as a .duty dictated merely by reason ; while the good works of Christians sprang from hearts which had been purified from sin and become temples of the Holy Ghost. Christians loved their brethren because they were all, potentially at least, the children of God and redeemed by Christ. The heart of man, when transformed by grace and indwelt by God cannot but be rich in creative thoughts and superhuman sacrifices.[1]

The Incarnation transformed and exalted the conception of human nature. Our divine Saviour in his practice and teaching looked upon man as the creature of God and thus gave him eternal value. He was not one of those simple enthusiasts who make a religion of the service of humanity as an end in itself. He was interested in humanity as part and parcel of God's purpose. Nietzsche remarked that in loving men for God's sake he achieved the most sublime and exalted sentiment that has ever been attained.[2]

The Gospel of Christ also revolutionized men's ideas on marriage and sexual morality. It is a decided exaggeration to say that the Fathers of the Church pronounced a curse upon sex, stigmatized women as the instruments of Satan, and poured scorn upon motherhood. Sceptical writers allege that such was the teaching of Origen, Saint Jerome, Saint Ambrose and Saint Augustine. The most that could

[1] Abbé Fouard, *St. Peter*, p. 331.
[2] Karl Adam, *Christ Our Brother*, p. 26.

[19]

be said is that these Fathers stressed the inferiority of the marriage state to virginity. Marriage as a remedy for concupiscence seemed to them a kind of concession (though lawful) to the wickedness of fallen nature. That is why they seem at times to talk rather strongly against marriage.

The teaching of the Church on such matters is not based so much upon revelation as upon reason. Mr. Christopher Dawson in his little book on *Christianity and Sex*, well says: "The Church has always based its teaching on marriage and sexual morality not on its ideals of asceticism nor even on its theological dogmas, but on broad grounds of natural law and social function." [1]

Saint Augustine, in his treatise *De Bono Conjugali*, wrote: "What food is to the conservation of the individual that sexual intercourse is to the conservation of the race." Mr. Dawson comments on this statement: "In so far as the sexual appetite is directed to its true end, it is as healthy and good as the desire for food. But on the other hand any attempt on the part of the individual to separate the pleasure which he derives from the satisfaction of sexual appetite, from its social purpose, is essentially immoral."

[1] Page 12.

The purpose of sex being social, it requires a social organ for its fulfilment and that organ is the family. The union of man and wife, is according to Saint Augustine, "the first natural bond of human society." But as the procreation of children is not the sole end of marriage, he finds a second good in the relation of friendship between a man and his wife. Thus marriage serves the purpose of mutual help, "so that when the warmth of youth has passed away, there yet lives in full vigor the odor of charity between husband and wife." The Catholic Church has never ceased to teach that marriage has a spiritual as well as a physical foundation.

III

THE teachers of the new faith were not content with making woman the companion of man ; they made her his equal. Moreover, Christianity added a new luster to maidenhood and virginity, as well as to motherhood. The veneration rendered to Mary, both as virgin and mother, was from the earliest days of the Church a powerful factor in transforming the attitude of Christian men toward women — flowering ultimately in the mediaeval ideal of chivalry. Neither did the new religion overlook the woman who had sinned ; but following the example of Christ it showed a never failing compassion to every sin-stained penitent soul.

Against the background of the brilliant but reckless society of Augustan Rome, as revealed in the pages of Ovid, the ideals and practices of the obscure sect of Christians stood out in startling relief. To be sure Ovid was looked upon with disapproval by the Emperor Augustus. The poet in defending himself argued that he was not injuring the morals of the people of Rome inasmuch as he had dedicated his *Ars Amoris* to the *Libertinae*. The full contrast however between pagan society and the Church did not become evident until several centuries after Christ, when the Church had grown stronger.

Until the conversion of Constantine, Christians lived apart from the rest of the world. They were unknown because they were being persecuted. In the fourth century the Christian population had become so large as to be considered a menace to the Empire. To the intellectual and governing classes Christians appeared anti-social and unpatriotic, because they would not worship the Roman gods, and had cut themselves off from all the pleasant things of life. They were unpopular with the leaders and also with the bulk of the citizens because they would not join in the general cult of material pleasure and success.

Saint Augustine in his *City of God* gives us some idea of the crass materialism of pagan society at the close of the fourth century. Before his conversion, he had lived in the midst of that society. The picture he draws for us is not a pleasant one. "They do not trouble about the moral degradation of the Empire ; all that they ask is that it should be prosperous and secure. 'What concerns us,' they say, 'is that everyone should be able to increase his wealth so that he can afford a lavish expenditure and can keep the weaker in subjection. Let the poor serve the rich for the sake of their bellies and so that they can live in idleness under their protection, and let the rich use the poor as dependants and to enhance their prestige. . . Let the laws protect the rights of property and leave men's morals alone. Let there be plenty of public prostitutes for whosoever wants them, above all for those who cannot afford to keep mistresses of their own. Let there be gorgeous palaces and sumptuous banquets, where anybody can play and drink and gorge himself and be dissipated by day or night, as much as he pleases or is able. Let the noise of dancing be everywhere, and let the theatres resound with lewd merriment and with every kind of cruel and vicious pleasure. Let the man who dislikes these pleasures be regarded as a public enemy, and if he tries to interfere with them, let the mob be free to hound him to death. But as for the rulers who devote themselves to giving the people a good time, let them be treated as gods and worshipped accordingly. Only let them take care that neither war nor plague nor any other calamity may interfere with this reign of prosperity'."[1]

The difference in the married life of Christians and their pagan contemporaries in the early centuries of the Church has been thus described by a Roman writer whose name is lost: "Christians are not distinguished from the rest of mankind in land or speech or customs . . . they marry and have children like everyone else — but they do not expose their children. They have meals in common but not wives. They are in the flesh, but they do not live after the flesh. They continue on earth, but their citizenship is in Heaven."[2]

Under the decadent paganism of the fourth century, the women of the Greco-Roman world had gradually been reduced to an evil plight through divorce, polygamy, childlessness and the necessity of

---

[1] *De Civitate Dei*, II, xx, in "St. Augustine and His Age," in *A Monument to St. Augustine.*
[2] Quoted by Glover in *The Conflict of Religions in the Early Roman Empire*, p. 169.

supporting themselves. The Catholic Church set them free from this degradation by making them the equals of men. She also recalled men to the dignity of fatherhood, the headship of the family, respect for women and an enduring family life. No one who had tasted of the new freedom which had been brought into the world by Christianity, would have dreamed of returning to the irksome conditions from which they had been delivered.

The situation today in Europe and America is in many respects the reverse of what it was in the world of the dying Roman Empire. But our modern society, except in the sections which maintain Christian traditions is casting aside the moral standards and institutions inherited from a Catholic past. Thousands of people of Christian stock, whose ancestors were bred in the moral ideals of the Gospel, are throwing off, as they say, the shackles of Christian dogma and the inhibitions of Christian morality. They now boast of their new freedom to believe and do as they like. They are deserting the faith of their fathers for neo-paganism, which lacks the freshness and vigor of ancient paganism, just as in the fourth century people turned their backs on a decadent paganism and flocked into the Catholic Church.

SOME PRACTICAL ASPECTS OF MYSTICAL EXPERIENCE

I

IN the course of a week's visit to Downside Abbey in September 1932, I had the happy privilege of a long talk with the Abbot, Dom John Chapman, on the subject of mystical experience. It would be more accurate to say that I prodded him with questions and that he did most of the talking. I had been struggling for some time to grasp Baron Von Hügel's conception of the essential nature of mysticism as set forth in his two-volume work on *The Mystical Element of Religion*. As I had found his exposition baffling, I was relieved to hear Dom Chapman say that he never could make out what Von Hügel was driving at on this particular subject.

Dom Chapman's explanation of the mystical faculty, which gives one facility in the prayer of contemplation, appealed to me so strongly that I immediately read his article "What is Mysticism?" in the *Downside Review* for January 1928, and his learned contribution on "Mysticism" in Hasting's *Encyclopedia of Religion and Ethics.*

In his *Spiritual Letters,* which have just been published, it becomes evident that he had apparently made it his business to test his theory of contemplative prayer, which he had arrived at mainly by *a priori* reasoning, by questioning a large number of contemplative monks and nuns, also a few persons living in the world, in regard to their method of prayer.

I shall try to set forth Dom Chapman's theory as I understand it without attempting to pronounce a critical judgment upon it. In my subsequent remarks on the frequency of the mystical state and its relations to active life I lean more heavily on Baron Von Hügel.

II

A CONNECTION always exists between any soul which is in the state of grace and God. However, what differentiaties the mystical from the non-mystical soul is the fact that the former is actually *conscious* of that connection, whereas the latter only knows it by faith or by inference. The means of communication between God and the soul may be compared to a wireless. This mystical faculty of the soul is neither natural nor supernatural. It comes under the head of the preternatural ; for it is beyond the ordinary human powers which we employ in our daily sense experience. It corresponds to the possession of a faculty in the soul which allows for the reception or a preternatural wave length of transmission from lesser realities, leading up to and inclusive of the Supreme Reality, God.

Such a faculty may be : (1) used in accordance with its ultimate end ; (2) disused ; (3) misused (i.e. not for the purpose of its ultimate end); (4) abused (i.e. against its ultimate end).

In the case of (1) the soul becomes conscious of the existence of the faculty and will use and develop it for the purpose of an ever-increasing union with a personal God. Such a person will become a true mystic.

In the case of (2) the soul will remain unconscious of the existence of the faculty, or if vaguely aware of it through "haphazard" transmissions, will ignore it, and may thus atrophy the faculty altogether.

In the case of (3) the soul will be aware of the faculty but will not use it in the right direction — i.e. towards a personal God. Such a person may develop into a nature-mystic, or become an artist or musician.

In the case of (4) a soul will be aware of the faculty but will use it in connection with some form of occultism developing possibly into communications with evil spirits.

There is reason for believing that this preternatural faculty, rare as it is, belongs inherently to human nature. It appears to be strong in unspoiled children; and it is more obvious in country children than in those compelled to live in cities. Shepherds, mountaineers and sailors are more likely to possess it than factory-workers, chauffeurs or financiers. Most people lose it as they grow older, either through simple disuse or by allowing it to be paralyzed by the noise and tumult of the world.

There are two ways of knowing : the ordinary way of sense impression, working upon the intellect and imagination ; and the extraordinary way of direct apprehension, without the intervention of the senses or the reasoning process. The mystical faculty enables one to apprehend reality independently of the senses and the discursive reason. It bears some resemblance to the means which the angels rely upon for their knowledge, as they are without bodies and therefore not dependent on the senses.

It has been thought by some that our first parents possessed this intuitional faculty before the fall. Through it they knew God directly, as the angels do. Their nature was in equilibrium ; their senses, imagination and emotions were perfectly subject to the will. This equilibrium was maintained by divine help. After they sinned, this help was forfeited both for them and their descendants. That is why the natural man, born in original sin, finds his higher faculties impeded by the lower. Sanctifying grace, however, can so far restore the balance that the higher part of our nature may be set free from the tyranny of the senses; and in contemplation holy souls may have glimpses of God. If we can only stimulate this preternatural faculty, the roots of which are in all of us, we may have a share in mystical experience.

We must, however, be on our guard against false mystics, whose name is legion. We can avoid the pitfalls of false mysticism by following only those guides who have been approved by the Catholic Church: such masters of mystical theology as Saint John of the Cross, Saint Teresa of Avila or Saint Francis de Sales.

Mystical theologians tell us that the mystical faculty, after it has been quickened and strengthened by sanctifying grace, can best be developed in silence and solitude. Idle talk, the telephone and the radio soon reduce to impotence this preternatural faculty of the soul. In addition there is need of mortification and contempt of the world, the adoption of approved means for the conquest of self, and the utilization of every opportunity for the prayer of contemplation. It is in the direction of self-discipline and mortification that people living in the world are most likely to fall short. God must be sought in the darkness, by abstraction from the objects of sense, by acts of faith in the unseen and eternal. There can be no true mystical life in one who has not cultivated the natural and supernatural virtues, entered upon the way of penitence, and learned the meaning of abstinence and self-control. Saint Benedict, in his monastic rule, laid down these conditions as essential for mystical progress : separation from the world, obedience, silence, and — above all — humility and perfect charity.

One of the classic statements of the requisites for mystical contemplation is to be found in the treatise on *Mystical Theology* by the writer known as the Pseudo-Dionysius: "And thou, dear Timothy, in thy intent practice of mystical contemplation, leave behind both thy senses and thy intellectual operations, and all things known by sense and intellect, and all things which are not and which are, and set thyself, as far as may be, to unite thyself in unknowing with him who is above all being and knowledge ; for by being purely free and absolute, out of self and of all things, thou shalt be led up to *the ray of the divine darkness*, stripped of all and loosed from all."

Saint Thomas holds that the quickening of this faculty of mystical vision is effected by the first two of the infused gifts of the Holy Ghost : wisdom and understanding. They restore to us some measure of the direct knowledge of God which human nature enjoyed at the beginning. These gifts establish in us a certain affinity to the divine.

Extraordinary mystical phenomena—ecstasy, levitation and the like—are not essential to the mystical experience. They are accidental physical accompaniments of the exercise of the mystical faculty in certain individuals ; but they are of no real value. Ecstasy is a trance-like state which is sometimes brought on by intense spiritual concentration. The other faculties remain dormant ; and it often seems as if they were tied and bound to keep them from acting. Mystical theologians apply to this mysterious force which binds the faculties the term ligature.

Ecstasy is more common in women than in men ; and in holy men of average intellect like Saint Joseph of Cupertino than in strong-minded saints like Saint Francis de Sales or Saint Vincent de Paul. It is worth noting that Saint John of the Cross insists that none of these phenomena are to be desired or prayed for ; and that if they occur, no attention is to be paid to them. We may conclude that it is proper to desire the grace of mystical prayer, but not its extraordinary by-products or psycho-physical effects.

The innate mystical gift, if reinforced by grace, may develop into real supernatural contemplative prayer ; if not so reinforced, it may become mere nature mysticism such as is found in many of the greater poets like Wordsworth or Tennyson. Probably also the leading musical composers owe much to the innate mystical sense ; and only those who possess this sense, in however slight a degree, can appreciate the higher kinds of music.

III

WHAT shall we say concerning the frequency of the mystical state ? In the average run of human beings the mystical sense is completely smothered in early childhood ; only in a few favored individuals may it be said to lie dormant, so that it can easily be awakened. These individuals may become poets, artists, or musicians, they may become religious mystics. They may even become both poets and saints.

Where the mystical faculty exists, it is exposed to

dangers from two opposite directions. It may be crowded out by the predominance of the emotional element in one's life, leading to an inordinate indulgence in anger, ambition, pleasure or love. Or it may be destroyed by exclusive reliance on the intellect. Thus the warm-hearted, jovial, type of person might often find it difficult to rise to heights of mystical contemplation ; and so would the coldly intellectual type, with starved emotional life. The type of psycho-physical organism which is conducive to mystical development is frequently found in philosophers, musicians and poets. Kant, Beethoven and Goethe are good examples of the type. Its characteristics are an intense spiritual energy, an extraordinary power of concentration on a single task and an extreme sensitiveness to suggestion.[1]

The great mystics have not been idle dreamers ; they have been the supreme spiritual geniuses of the race. Grounded in humility and possessed by divine charity, their lives have been characterized by spiritual fruitfulness and practical ingenuity. Each has been dominated by some truth of immense importance to themselves and the world. Ezekiel was absorbed in vast prophetic schemes for the safeguarding of the chosen people. Saint Paul became

[1] Von Hügel, *Mystical Element in Religion*, vol. II, "Psychophysical Problems."

an indefatigable missionary to the Gentile world.
Saint Francis of Assisi, through his love of poverty,
saved civilization from corruption. Saint Catherine
of Siena inspired the papacy to set itself free from
the French domination. Saint Joan of Arc delivered
her nation from the English yoke. Saint Teresa and
Saint John of the Cross reformed the great Carmelite
order.

While the cloistered life is more conducive to the
exercise of the mystical faculty than life in the world
and in the married state, the active life is by no
means incompatible with contemplation. This is
proved by the fact that God has given to married
saints many mystical favors, for example to such
saints as Queen Margaret of Scotland, Saint Louis
of France, Saint Elizabeth of Hungary, Saint Catherine of Genoa, Blessed Anna Maria Taigi, or
Blessed Nicholas of Flüe. The quieting of concupiscence in married life may even be in many cases
a positive aid to contemplation. Although the absorbing care of children and the distracting duties of
the home tend to make contemplation more difficult
for married women than for their husbands, there
are many wives and mothers who have so organized
their lives that they have surmounted this obstacle.
Saint Gregory the Great said that the mystical life
was possible for those living in the world and in the

married state ; and that the active life may assist the contemplative, provided that tranquillity of mind is not too much impeded.[1]

The Catholic Church in all ages has consistently opposed the teaching that the material and the spiritual, the body and the soul, are necessarily antagonistic to each other. She never encouraged the neo-Platonic tendency to look upon the body and its functions as obstacles to the free working of the spirit. God made the material as well as the spiritual part of man's nature ; and what God made cannot be inherently evil. The problem for every man is not how to ignore or suppress his bodily nature ; but how best to utilize it for rational, moral and spiritual ends. This is in accordance with the principles of sound psychology, which stresses the close union and constant interaction of body and soul.

Saint Thomas was a true humanist in his defence of the body. He taught that the soul was the determining and active principle of the body. Man is not pure spirit, like the angels ; nor purely material, like the animals. He is both in one. "It is not our body which feels, nor our mind which thinks ; but we, as single human beings, who feel and think." [2] It could not have seen said of Saint

[1] Dom Chapman, "Mysticism" in Hasting's *Encyclopedia of Religion and Ethics.*

[2] M. C. D'Arcy, S.J., *Saint Thomas*, p. 207.

Thomas that he hated to be a man. He said that "man is bound by a kind of natural debt to live with others merrily." He held that even if man had not fallen, the race would have multiplied through the natural process of generation.

The Church has been equally insistent on our maintaining a right relationship to the society of human beings in which we live. We must use the world as not abusing it. The Catholic ideal is neither complete detachment, nor entire absorption by the world and its interests ; but rather a perfect balance between detachment and attachment. If one is stressed at the expense of the other, it leads to an unwholesome abnormality on which the Church would refuse to put her seal of approval. The great mystics have been detached from worldly possessions and ambitions, crucified with Christ to the concupiscence of the flesh and of the eyes, and to the pride of life ; such detachment, however, always had for its object a greater attachment, and has enabled them to throw themselves with immense energy into necessary human activities, and in consequence to transform and spiritualize their environment and their age.

We learn both from the lives of the Catholic mystics, and from the opposition to Manicheanism which the Catholic Church has maintained through the ages, that it is wrong to attack the family, society, the state, art, literature or science, as things intrinsically evil or in any way obstacles to moral and religious perfection. On the contrary, they must all be utilized for higher ends. The spiritual life must have something to work upon, just as the leaven must be mixed with dough. So these wider human interests furnish the materials, occasions and objects for Christian spirituality to raise to a higher order, and thereby to become strengthened and deepened itself. Divine grace does not function in a vacuum.

This point has been elaborated in the second volume of Von Hügel's *Mystical Element in Religion*.[1] He goes on to make further observations as to the relative advantages of the monastic and the married state for contemplation. He says that it looks as if the Church, by her canonization of the monastic ideal, had given us the only means by which the soul might flee from the body and the world. But we must remember that "the Church not only forbids all attacks upon the legitimacy, indeed sanctity, of marriage, or upon its necessity, indeed duty, for mankind at large ; but Saint Augustine and Saint Thomas only articulate her ordinary, anti-Manichean teaching, in declaring that man was originally created by God, in body and in soul, not for celibacy, but

[1] Vol. II, pp. 126-8.

for marriage ; and that only owing to the accidental event of the fall and its effects — the introduction of disorder and excess into human nature, but not any corruption of its substance and foundations — does any infirmity attach to marriage as compared with virginity."

SAINT MONICA
[331-387]

I

When still a young girl, Monica gained her first spiritual victory. She was frequently sent to the cellar to fetch wine for the family's use. She tasted it and found she liked it; soon she required a glassful to quench her thirst. The servants discovered her secret, and once in a moment of temper one of them called her a "winebibber." She made a vow that from that day she would drink nothing but water. She adhered to that resolution to the end of her life. We learn later from the sermons of Augustine that over-indulgence in wine was one of the besetting sins of the women of Africa.

In the earlier years of her married life she found that her pagan husband, Patricius, was a man of uncontrollable temper. Her mother-in-law was also a pagan, and usually sided with the husband in his outbursts of wrath. She stirred up further trouble by telling false tales to the servants about Monica, who met all their insults with silence. It appears to have been the custom, among the male citizens of Tagaste, when they quarreled with their wives, to disfigure their faces with bruises. These ladies often appeared in the market-place bearing these marks of domestic infelicity. They were amazed that Monica never displayed such signs of ill-treatment, and pleaded with her to divulge her method of dealing with an irate husband.

One day Monica confided to a group of these women her nostrum for taming a fierce husband: "Guard your tongue when your husband is in passion."

As the years went on, Monica's meekness and humility, together with her prayers, had a transforming effect upon Patricius. He was given the grace of faith and one year at the beginning of Lent had himself enrolled among the catechumens. The formal relationship that had hitherto existed between husband and wife developed into a warm spiritual devotion to each other. Soon after his baptism he fell ill, and after several months of acute suffering, when his wife attended him day and night, he finally died in peace and joy.

Augustine was not baptized in infancy. He was carried to the church, where the sign of the cross was marked on his forehead, and he was inscribed as a catechumen. In his boyhood his mother often spoke to him of the love of God, and tried to explain to him the principles of her faith. Writing later of this period of his life in his *Confessions*, he says : "I myself had then the gift of faith, so had every one in the house except my father, but he never was able to weaken the influence of my mother, which was so overpowering from the force of her example, that he could not succeed in turning me away from a firm belief in the Savior whom he ignored."

After her husband died, Monica made a vow that her life in the future should belong wholly to God. She renounced all worldly pleasures. What time she could spare from her duties at home she spent in ministering to the needs of the poor, especially by providing for the spiritual nurture of orphan children.

There was one task, however, which she considered had the first claim on her time and attention, and that was the conversion of her impetuous and wayward son Augustine. While he was still under the tutelage of one of the ablest masters in Tagaste, her husband had let her know that the boy had now become a man and had fallen into evil ways. To be sure he was only sixteen, but a boy of sixteen in Africa was as mature as a man of twenty-one in the north of Europe. Apparently he indulged in all the vices common to the boys of his age. His mother pleaded with him to forsake his sinful habits, but without result. As he wrote later, "My mother's words appeared to me only those of a woman who knew nothing of the world . . . thus I despised her gentle warnings, or rather I despised God, who was speaking to me through her."

II

AFTER attending a school at Madaura, six miles from Tagaste, Augustine was sent to the university at Carthage. Because of the family's poverty, Romanianus, a rich citizen of Tagaste, agreed to meet the expenses of his education. Monica hoped that the study of science and philosophy would open his mind to the truth and lead him back to God. She did not reckon on the other accompaniments of a sojourn in Carthage.

In that city of philosophy and dancing girls, of favorite jockeys and obscene religion, Augustine soon found that he was "ridiculous if innocent ; despicable if pure — the greatest shame of all was to feel ashamed." He became a member of a club which boasted the formidable title *Eversores* — implying that they were against the established order.

In the midst of this seething mass of iniquity, Augustine became infatuated with a young woman,

[43]

whose name he never reveals, and for the next fifteen years he remained faithful to her. She gave birth to a son, upon whom Augustine bestowed the name Adeodatus—"Given by God." His love for this one woman and for his son became a stabilizing influence in his life, and rendered him more human and civilized.

Along with his other experiments in Carthage, he explored the latest heresy. He publicly renounced the Catholic faith, and declared that he had joined the sect of the Manichees. He persuaded many of his young friends to follow his example. This sect appealed to the young because of its teaching that all matter was evil, the flesh was to be despised, and bodily actions had no moral significance. The Manichean doctrine of evil brought relief to Augustine's troubled soul. He could not escape the feeling that his life was all wrong. It consoled him to believe that the evil principle resided *in* a man without being *of* him. "Something sins within me ; it is not I who sin."

When this fervent young convert to Manicheism returned to Tagaste for his vacation, he was astounded to hear his mother order him to leave her home and never enter it again till he had renounced his errors and submitted to the truth. "Very harsh and narrow-minded," many moderns would say.

"Why not let him live his own life, and discover the truth in his own way? There is good in all religions. If he finds Manicheism spiritually helpful, why not be tolerant and wish him God-speed?"

It was not Monica's way. She was a persistent woman, who would not permit her son's life to be devastated by a false philosophy and vain deceit. She loved her son intensely and she knew he had a brilliant mind and a magnetic personality. Perhaps she dreamed that one day they would be employed in the service of God.

It was her invincible faith — not only in God, but in Augustine — that saved him for greater things. It would have been an irreparable loss to the Church and the world if she had been content to let him marry and settle down as a mediocre teacher of rhetoric in Carthage and a pillar in the Manichean temple. Monica must have had an intuition that such was not the will of God. There is a moment in every man's life when he stands at the crossways. His correspondence with the will of God and his future usefulness depend on his taking the right turn. That Augustine did not commit himself irrevocably to the wrong road was due to his mother's firmness and vision at this critical time.

After completing his studies, Augustine opened a school of oratory in Carthage. He also began to gather disciples whom he instructed in the principles of Manicheism. He had now discovered that the Manicheans were more adept in attacking the Catholic faith than in establishing the truth of their own theories. The death of an intimate friend plunged him into melancholy. In such a juncture his new religion was powerless to help him.

Just then Faustinus, an aged Manichean bishop, arrived in Carthage. Augustine had been anxiously awaiting his coming and propounded to him at once some of his intellectual difficulties. The modest old man confessed that he could suggest no solution for his problems. This had a distinctly chilling effect on Augustine's enthusiasm.

About this time Monica had a dream. In her dream she was standing on a narrow plank, and Augustine came and stood beside her, saying, "Where you are, I am." When she told the dream to Augustine, he argued that it meant that she would become a Manichean; but she insisted that it was he who would one day stand where she had always stood.

She kept on praying for her son's conversion. Prayers and tears — such were her arguments; the dynamic behind them was an inextinguishable love. As La Rochefoucauld says, "Love is like a flame; it can never be still, and dies when it ceases to hope or to fear." Monica's love would never cease to hope. One day she went to a holy bishop in Carthage — whose name we do not know — and pleaded with him to make an effort to save her son. The bishop was himself a convert from Manicheism, and that may have been her reason for consulting him. There was deep wisdom in his famous reply : "Go thy ways and God be with thee ; it is not possible that the son of these tears should perish."

For seventeen years Monica pleaded with God that her son might be given the grace of conversion. At the same time she pursued the young man relentlessly, like Francis Thompson's Hound of Heaven, from Tagaste to Carthage, from Carthage to Rome, from Rome to Milan. She must have attracted attention, for she wore the purple veil and long white habit of a consecrated widow, which she had received from her bishop after her husband died, in token of her renunciation of the world. To give added power to her prayer, she fasted. Holy Communion was her daily food, and she was often favored with the grace of ecstasy.

III

AUGUSTINE, having become disgusted with the young men of Carthage because of their frivolity, decided

[47]

to try his fortune in Rome. He deceived his mother about his plans and slipped away from Carthage in the night. Shortly after his arrival at Rome he was taken seriously ill and nearly died, but still he did not ask for baptism. On recovering, he opened his school of oratory.

Monica had heard that Rome was a hotbed of paganism and vice, so she thought it advisable to follow him. The depressed tone of his letters added to her anxiety. To arrange for the journey to Rome, she was compelled to sell her few remaining possessions. In the meantime Augustine had found that his Roman pupils did not pay their fees promptly, and some not at all. Perhaps that accounted for the gloom in his letters.

Then came an unlooked for opening. Symmachus, the prefect of Rome, had received a request to appoint a new professor of rhetoric for a chair that had just fallen vacant in Milan. He himself was a well-known orator, and in the competition for the new post he was the judge. Augustine won the coveted prize, in spite of his African accent. The letter in which he announced the good news to his mother never reached her. The post in this part of the world has never been dependable. Thus it happened that when she arrived in Rome after her long tiresome journey, she heard that he had gone to Milan. She permitted herself only a day's rest in Rome, and then set out to cross the Apennines with Milan as her destination.

One of the first visits Augustine had made in Milan was to the Bishop Ambrose. It was a necessary courtesy for one who had been appointed to a professorial chair in that city. From the start he felt strongly attracted to Ambrose as to a kindred spirit. The bishop received him with fatherly kindness, as he bore letters of introduction from Symmachus, an old friend of Ambrose.

Augustine soon came to love the bishop as a father, and went every Sunday to study Ambrose the orator and hear him expound the Scriptures. He had by this time begun to see the folly of Manicheism, and its gross misrepresentation of the Catholic Church ; but he could not yet believe in the Church. He had attained the age of thirty, and was thoroughly sophisticated and disillusioned with the world. When he learned that his mother had arrived in Milan, he was not annoyed that she had followed him.

She too made her first visit in Milan to the Bishop Ambrose. They understood each other at a glance. A few days later the bishop said to Augustine, "Thank God for having given you such a mother ; she is one in a thousand."

Monica now learned that her son had become disgusted with Manicheism ; and they attended church
together, as they had when he was a boy, and afterwards discussed the sermons of the bishop.   Monica
had made a deep study of philosophy and theology,
in order that she might be able to deal intelligently
with her son's difficulties.   The Manicheans had
sneered at faith as childish ; but now he began to
realize how many things he believed that he could
not prove but accepted on the testimony of others.

We may see an answer to the prayers of Monica
in the ordering of events that thus brought her son
under the influence of so wise and holy a director
and guide as Ambrose.   Conversions are rarely
brought about through an immediate influx of divine
grace, but through the agency of events and persons.

Monica made use of every wile known to mothers
to bring her son into personal contact with the bishop.
For example, one day she sent him to ask the bishop
what she was to do about the Saturday fast, which
was observed in Africa but not in Milan.   Augustine
brought back to her the famous reply which has since
become the rule for Catholics everywhere : "Follow
the custom of the Church where you are.   If you
are at Rome, fast with the Church of Rome ; but if
you are at Milan, do not fast when the Church of
Milan does not do so."

On another occasion she was taking to the church a basket of bread, wine and meats, which according to the custom among the faithful in Africa she was about to offer on the altar of the saint whose festival was being celebrated. She was turned away from the church door by a messenger from the bishop, who forbade her to enter the church with her basket. This custom had been discontinued in Milan owing to the abuses to which it had given rise. She meekly bowed her head, and immediately sought out some poor families who might make use of the food.

The critical moment had now come in the career of Augustine. He must choose between God and the mistress who had been dominating his life for so many years. Ambrose had persistently refused to argue with him on matters of faith, because he knew — as Monica knew — that he was no longer being held back by intellectual difficulties, but by the necessity of choosing between human and divine love.

Augustine was given the grace to make the sacrifice. We can only guess what this meant to the mother of his son, who had to leave him forever, and begin her penitential discipline in a convent. We do know what it meant to Augustine. He describes this turning point in his life in one poignant sentence : "I allowed myself to be turned from her who shared my life, and as my soul was one with hers my riven heart shed tears of blood."

IV

MEANWHILE a group of friends had gathered round Augustine in Milan. They set apart a certain time every day to read together, especially from the Scriptures, and to search for the truth. Augustine wrote : "Great hope has dawned ; the Catholic faith teaches not what we thought and vainly accused it of. Life is vain, death uncertain ; if it steals upon us of a sudden, in what state shall we depart hence ? And where shall we learn what here we have neglected ? Let us not delay to seek after God and the blessed life."

An aged priest, Simplicianus, narrated to him the courageous conversion of old Victorinus, whose translation of Plato he had been reading ; and this made him conscious of his own cowardice. Although he believed that the Catholic Church was the true Church, he could not bring himself to make the renunciations which baptism implied. Pontitianus told him of the life of Saint Anthony the Hermit, and of how two men of the imperial court had been converted by reading his life and became recluses. Their moral heroism increased Augustine's self-reproach, and leaving his friends he rushed into the garden. Alypius followed him.

"What are we about?" exclaimed Augustine. "The unlearned take heaven by force, and we, with all our heartless learning, wallow in the mire!" A bitter struggle was going on in his soul. It seemed as if he saw a long procession of saints of all ages winding slowly across the garden and looking at him reproachfully.

He turned from Alypius and walked to the other end of the garden, where he threw himself on the ground and wept, crying out to God for help. Suddenly the stillness of the summer afternoon was broken by a child's voice chanting the words *"Tolle, lege,"* again and again. "Take and read," was doubtless the answer to his prayer. He arose quickly and went back to Alypius and opened the scroll of Saint Paul's Epistles, that lay on the table.

These were the words that first struck his eye: "Put ye on the Lord Jesus Christ, and make not provision for the flesh and the concupiscence thereof." Alypius too opened the book and read, "He that is weak in the faith take unto you," and declared that would do very well for him.

Augustine went at once to Monica and told her what had happened, and how his old life had dropped from him like a garment. He threw himself into her arms. At last her long agony was ended! We can only faintly imagine what the embrace of that mother and son meant to both of them. They sat together in silence hand in hand while the sun slowly sank behind the rose-colored clouds in the golden west, and the cool shadows lengthened.

From his *Confessions* we learn how much of his conversion he attributed to her: "It is to my mother that I owe all." "If I am thy child, O my God, it is because thou gavest me such a mother." "If I prefer the truth to all other things, it is the fruit of my mother's teaching." "If I did not long ago perish in sin and misery, it is because of the long and faithful tears with which she pleaded for me."

When the period of his instruction was over, Augustine was baptized by Ambrose in the church in Milan on Holy Saturday, 387, in the presence of his mother and his faithful friends.

In the light of fifteen centuries of Catholic history, we may now evaluate the life and work of Saint Monica. Leaving out of our reckoning the conversion of her husband, can we overestimate the worth of her achievement in gaining for her son the gift of faith? She thereby bequeathed to the Catholic Church perhaps the keenest philosophical mind, the most comprehenseive theologian, the most persuasive apologist, and the most far-seeing moralist in all her company of bishops, confessors, and doctors. A wise administrator, a powerful preacher, and a penetrating mystic, his writings still influence millions of readers. Countless religious, men and women, in all parts of the world, are today living under the Augustinian Rule.

Soon afterwards, Augustine and his friends — who had also become Catholics — decided to return to Africa. Monica accompanied them on the journey to Ostia, whence they were to embark. Her work in this world was accomplished and she longed to depart for her true home.

Augustine tells in his *Confessions* of their mystical converse with one another : "It fell out, as I believe, through thy Providence working in thy hidden ways, that she and I, alone together, were standing leaning upon a certain window, from which there was a view of the garden within the house that sheltered us, there at Ostia on the Tiber, where apart from the throng, after the fatigue of our long journey, we were recruiting ourselves for our voyage. Together we two held converse very sweet, and forgetting those things which were behind, and reaching forth into those things that were before, we were discussing between us, in the presence of the Truth which thou art, of what kind would be that eternal life of the saints. . . . Our counsel drew to such an end that the utmost delight of the bodily senses in the clearest material light, by the side of the enjoyment of that life, seemed unworthy . . . even to be named with it. . . . On that day when we were speaking of such things and this world with all its delights, amid such converse, was beginning to grow but cheap to us, then said she, 'My son, as for myself, I delight no longer in anything in this life. What yet here I may do, and why I linger here, I know not, now that the hope of this life has died within me. There was but one thing for which I longed to tarry here a while, that I might see thee a Catholic Christian before my death. And this my God hath given me even more abundantly, so that I even see thee his servant, and able to despise mere earthly happiness. What do I here?'"

She told him to lay her body anywhere, but to remember her at the Lord's altar wherever he might be. Nine days later she died, in the fifty-sixth year of her age and the thirty-third year of Augustine's. They buried her in Ostia, whence her sacred relics were translated a thousand years later by Pope Martin V to the Church of Saint Augustine in Rome.

SAINT PAULINUS OF NOLA
[353-431]

I

PONTIUS MEROPIUS ANICIUS PAULINUS was born of a noble Roman family near Bordeaux in Aquitania about the middle of the fourth century. His father was pretorian prefect in Gaul and owned extensive landed property in Aquitania and Italy. Up to his fifteenth year the boy received a many-sided literary training under the poet Ausonius, who was half pagan, half Christian. There is no evidence that Ausonius tried to convert him to Christianity. Until his tutor died, Paulinus held him in high esteem.

In his fifteenth year, Pontius Meropius went to the University of Bordeaux, where he studied Roman law, poetry, eloquence, science and the Platonic philosophy. He was not at that time attracted to a life of piety. He looked forward to easy and happy years, as was natural for a Roman gentleman who was to inherit vast wealth and would presumably enjoy a distinguished career.

When his father died, he was only twenty-four;

but his habits were such that the inheritance of large estates with numerous villas and many slaves did not prevent him from continuing to live the restrained life of a humanist and man of letters.

As one of the richest proprietors of the Empire, he was called upon at once to fulfil important public functions ; and in his twenty-fifth year he became a senator. In the same year the Emperor Gratian, probably under the advice of Ausonius, who had also been his tutor in his youth, nominated Pontius Meropius to fill the unexpired term of one of the Consuls of Rome. The young man went to Rome and was initiated into office with the customary pomp and vested with the rich costume of the consuls. He was applauded by the populace and congratulated by his friends.

The next year he was appointed governor of Campania, and took up his abode in Nola, in the mountains east of Naples, where he had inherited a large estate. It speaks well for his pagan training that these honors did not turn the head of so young a man. Paulinus was apparently devoid of vanity, and cared little for the applause of men. His literary and philosophical education had already convinced him of the emptiness of worldly honors and pleasures.

His first year in Nola was decisive in his life as a

man and a Christian. On the feast day of Saint
Felix, the patron saint of Campania, when the
faithful flocked from all the countryside to Nola
and crowded into the church to offer their devotions
at his shrine, Paulinus saw something that disturbed
his equilibrium as a pagan philosopher. He saw
several sick people healed at the tomb of the saint.
At that moment he felt in his soul the first stirrings
of divine grace. Looking back in later years to this
experience, he attributed to it the first impulse toward his conversion.

In one of the many poems which he wrote on the
recurring feast days of Saint Felix, he thus describes
this beginning of his conversion : "Young Gaul that
I was from the shores of the West, I had barely with
trembling feet touched the threshold of thy sanctuary, when I beheld the marvels that were wrought
before the door of the church which enshrines thy
mortal body, which still radiates after thy virtue.
With all the powers of my soul I adhered to the
true faith, and it was in thy light that my heart first
opened to the love of Christ."

He sealed his new determination with a peculiar
ceremony, pagan at least in its origin. He sacrificed
his first beard to Saint Felix. Thereupon he resigned his post as governor, and returned to Aquitania where his mother was impatiently awaiting him.

Shortly after his return to Aquitania, he made a journey into Spain, and thence brought home with him a wife, Theresa by name. She was of an honorable Iberian family, and brought as her dowry properties almost as extensive as her husband's. She was a strong-minded woman, and when she was once convinced that a course of action was right, no emotional considerations could make her deviate from her duty. She bore throughout a long life most worthily the name that was later to be glorified by the greatest of Spanish mystics.

In one of his later poems on Saint Felix' Day, Paulinus intimates that she became a Christian before he did, though whether she was a Christian at the time of their marriage we do not know. He thus refers to his marriage : "As a stranger I crossed the Pyrenees, and came to the neighboring land of the Iberians. There Thou didst permit that I take a wife according to human laws ; thus Thou didst gain at the same time two lives, and madest use of the yoke of the flesh to secure together the salvation of two souls ; and by the merits of the woman, Thou didst compensate for the hesitations of the man." He made several sojourns of some length in Spain with his wife, to look after her property.

For four years his old tutor, Ausonius, received no answers to the poems he had addressed to Pauli-

nus. The poems which Paulinus wrote him in return, through some mishap to the post, never reached
him; and for an old man of seventy, four years is
a long time to wait for a letter. Ausonius, in another poem made some caustic remarks about the
wife whom Paulinus had taken, thinking that she
had dissuaded him from answering. Thereupon
Paulinus sent to his old friend this lyrical outburst:

I, through all chances that are given to mortals,
    And through all fates that be,
So long as this close prison shall contain me,
    Yea, though a world shall sunder me and thee,

Thee shall I hold, in every fibre woven,
    Not with dumb lips, nor with averted face
Shall I behold thee, in my mind embrace thee,
    Instant and present, thou, in every place.

Yea, when the prison of this flesh is broken,
    And from the earth I shall have gone my way,
Wheresoe'er in the wide universe I stay me,
    There shall I bear thee, as I do today.

Think not the end, that from my body frees me,
    Breaks and unshackles from my love to thee;
Triumphs the soul above its house in ruin,
    Deathless, begot of immortality.

Still must she keep her senses and affections,
    Hold them as dear as life itself to be.
Could she choose death, then might she choose
      forgetting;
    Living, remembering, to eternity.[1]

[1] Translation by Helen Waddell, *Mediaeval Latin Lyrics*, Constable
and Company, London, 1929, p. 37.

II

ALTHOUGH the work of divine grace, which finally resulted in the conversion of Paulinus, began when he was governor of Campania, it was not until ten years later, when he was thirty-six, that he was baptized by Saint Delphinus, the Bishop of Bordeaux. Many men, who afterwards became saints, were the instruments through which the grace of God operated upon him. Saint Martin of Tours miraculously cured him from an affliction of the eyes. He had many talks on religion with Saint Victricius, Bishop of Rouen; with Saint Delphinus, the bishop, and Saint Amandus, a priest of Bordeaux; and with his friend Sulpicius Severus, who became a Christian at about the same time. Above all it was Saint Ambrose, the Bishop of Milan, whose sermons finally led him to make the decision to place himself under his instruction. Possibly the example of Augustine's conversion, and his baptism by Ambrose in 387 — two years before his own baptism — was a powerful factor in moving his stubborn will.

He seems to have been converted by contagion. Though he nowhere mentions his wife as one of the influences leading him to become a Christian, it may have been because a Roman patrician of those days did not like to admit that he was being led by a woman, or because she influenced him by indirect methods of which he was not conscious. It is reasonable to assume that Theresa's prayers and merits were not without their effect upon her husband.

To readjust their lives to the new conditions demanded by his conversion, Paulinus and his wife went to Spain, where they remained for the next four years. Before their departure, Paulinus disposed of his estates in Gaul, selling some and giving the money to the poor, and dividing others among his slaves. Ausonius, now very aged, tried to dissuade him — in verse — from so precipitate a separation from the world :

> Let me not weep to see thy ravished house
> All sad and silent, without lord or spouse,
> And all those vast dominions, once thine own,
> Torn 'twixt a hundred slaves to me unknown !

This abandonment of his property was naturally regarded by all his old pagan friends as a base desertion of the Empire at a critical time in her history. There was then, as always, a sharp antagonism between the spirit of enjoyment and the spirit of renunciation — the claims of the world and the claims of God. Paulinus, at this turning point in his career, displayed an energy of will and enthusiasm which no opposition could abate.

Theresa his wife was not only willing for her

husband to make these sacrifices ; but as soon as they arrived in Spain, she sold her own lands and devoted the proceeds to the redemption of captives, and the setting free of debtors by paying their debts.

It was about this time that a son was born to Paulinus and Theresa, and died soon after baptism, when only eight days old. This calamity may have been due to the physical condition of the mother, and in consequence Paulinus may have felt that it would be an act of charity on his part if he relinquished his rights as a husband. Whatever the reason may have been, they both took the vows of chastity ; and henceforward lived under one roof as brother and sister.

It must have been at this juncture that Paulinus wrote to Ausonius one of his most beautiful lyrics, explaining to his beloved teacher why he had entered upon the path of heroic renunciation :

> Not that they beggared be in mind, or brutes,
> That they have chosen their dwelling-place afar
> In lonely places : but their eyes are turned
> To the high stars, the very deep of Truth.
> Freedom they seek, an emptiness apart
> From worthless hopes, din of the marketplace,
> And all the noisy crowding up of things,
> And whatsoever wars on the divine,
> At Christ's command and for his love, they hate ;
> By faith and hope they follow after God,

And know their quest shall not be desperate,
If but the Present conquer not their souls
With hollow things : that which they see they spurn
That they may come at what they do not see,
Their senses kindled like a torch, that may
Blaze through the secrets of eternity.
The transient's open, everlastingness
Denied our sight ; yet still by hope we follow
The vision that our minds have seen, despising
The shows and forms of things, the loveliness
Soliciting for ill our mortal eyes.
The present's nothing : but eternity
Abides for those on whom all truth, all good,
Hath shone, in one entire and perfect light.[1]

Three years after the baptism of Paulinus, while he was still sojourning in Spain, the populace of Barcelona — impressed no doubt by his sacrifice of his high imperial position and the distribution of his goods among the poor — laid hands upon him and carried him to the bishop, and begged that he would ordain this holy man to the priesthood. Paulinus would consent to ordination only on condition that he be bound to no parish or diocese. The bishop accepted the conditions and conferred holy orders upon him. His ordination was certainly irregular, but not invalid ; because he received it with free consent.

[1] Translation by Helen Waddell, *Mediaeval Latin Lyrics*, p. 35.

During the following year Paulinus and his "sister" set forth for Italy. On arriving at Milan, they became the guests of Saint Ambrose, who gave Paulinus instructions on the duties of his priestly office. Then they visited in Rome. Pope Siricius and the other authorities of the Roman Church received Paulinus somewhat coldly, whether because of the notoriety he had obtained through the surrender of his possessions, or because of the peculiar circumstances of his ordination, or because he appeared to have a wife,[1] or because of his friendship with Saint Martin of Tours who was then somewhat under suspicion of heresy — perhaps for all these reasons. He then proceeded to Nola, where he and Theresa lived henceforth a severely ascetic life near the tomb of his beloved Felix. It may be well to hear what two unimpeachable contemporary witnesses thought of the characters of Paulinus and Theresa:

In 394, Saint Augustine wrote a letter to Paulinus and Theresa at Nola, in which he expressed his admiration for a woman who, "far from serving as a guide to her husband in the ways of softness, has been led back by him to the virile energy typified by the bone from which the first woman was formed."

[1] Only about eight years before, in a letter to Bishop Himerius of Taragona, Pope Siricius had laid down seven regulations against married priests. Denzinger's *Enchiridion Symbolorum,* p. 89.

SAINT PAULINUS OF NOLA

Saint Ambrose, in his thirtieth Epistle to Sabinus writes as follows :

Paulinus, the most eminent for his nobility in all the parts of Aquitania, having sold away all his patrimonies, together with the goods of his wife, did out of pure love to Jesus Christ divide all that vast sum of money amongst the poor ; and he himself from a rich senator is become a most poor man, having cast off that heavy secular burden, and forsaken his own house, his country and his kindred, that he might with more earnestness follow Christ. His wife also, as nobly descended, and as zealous for the faith as himself, consented to all his desires, and having given away all her own large possessions, lives with her husband in a little thatched cottage, rich in nothing but the hidden treasures of religion and charity. As they have no children, they wish themselves to give their good works to posterity. When the senators shall learn of this, what shall they say ?   A man of such birth, of so great a family, of his character and eloquence — to abandon the Senate ! To interrupt the succession of a noble race !   That cannot be !   And these same men, who shave their hair and eyebrows if they are initiated into the mysteries of Isis, cry out against the indignity if any one changes his garment for the sake of the holy religion of Christ. So much consideration for falsehood and contempt for the truth ! "Whosoever shall be ashamed of me before men, of him shall I be ashamed before God."

III

ONE so familiar with the problems of the imperial government as Paulinus must have foreseen the rapidly approaching fall of the Empire in the West. He knew that the Vandals and Huns and other barbarian hordes were everywhere breaking through the frontiers of imperial defence ; and he could see that the moral fibre of the old pagan families was deteriorating. He could also see that the Catholic Church was increasing in vigor and extent, indeed that it was the only institution that possessed any vitality or power of renewal. Instead of remaining enmeshed in the dying civilization around him and lamenting its decay, he chose to make the great renunciation and attach himself to the invincible kingdom of Christ.

The world is always passing away, and it is one of the tragedies of human existence that so many men and women become entirely absorbed in this impermanent phantasmagoria of passing things, and blind to the eternal realities. Paulinus gave expression to this contrast in a memorable sentence : "And not only pagan literature, but the whole sensible appearance of things is the lotus flower ; so men forget their own land, which is God, the country of us all."

Only a few decades later, Saint Augustine, looking out upon the devastation which the Vandals were bringing upon the Province of Africa as they slowly came nearer to his see city of Hippo, wrote his great

SAINT PAULINUS OF NOLA

work, *The City of God,* in which he set forth his philosophy of history and his hopes for the new age which was to come.

He viewed all history as the evolution of two opposite principles embodied in two hostile societies, the heavenly and the earthly cities, Sion and Babylon, the Church and the World. The one had no final realization on earth, it was *in via,* its *patria* was heavenly and eternal ; the other found its realization in earthly prosperity, in the wisdom and glory of man ; it was its own end and its own justification. The State, it is true, was not condemned as such. In so far as it was Christian, it subserved the ends of the heavenly city. But it was a subordinate society, the servant and not the master : it was the spiritual society that was supreme. The moment that the State came ino conflict with the higher power, the moment that it set itself up as an end in itself, it became identified with the earthly city and lost all claims to a higher sanction than the law of force and self-interest. Without justice, what is a great kingdom but a great robbery — *magnum latrocinium ?* Conquering or being conquered does no one either good or harm. It is pure waste of energy, the game of fools for an empty prize. The terrestrial world is unsubstantial and transitory, the only reality worth striving for is that which is eternal — the heavenly Jerusalem — the "vision of peace." [1]

Paulinus and Theresa made their home at Nola in a hospice for the poor and sick, which they had founded when they sold their estates. Theresa

[1] Christopher Dawson, *The Making of Europe,* p. 192.

lived on the first floor and acted as matron for the hospice. On the second floor was a monastery, where Paulinus and other hermits established one of the first monastic centres in the West, a century before Saint Benedict ; and lived a life of severe asceticism. Their garments were of hair-cloth, with a rope girdle, and their heads were shaven. They observed strict rules of silence and fasting. They ate nothing till three in the afternoon, and their one meal consisted chiefly of vegetables. They slept on the floor under blankets made of patchwork ; but as they spent so little time in sleep, it did not greatly matter what was under them or what covered them.

Whether due to his severe life of self-mortification or to an inherent weakness of constitution, Paulinus was frequently ill. He took his ailments philosophically, maintaining that "the weakness of the body is advantageous to the spirit, which rejoices in the losses of the flesh." This was the view of illness which Pascal took many centuries later. Nevertheless, Paulinus lived to be seventy-eight.

Paulinus unbosomed himself to Sulpicius Severus more than to his other friends. In one of his letters to Sulpicius we are favored with a glimpse of his inner spiritual struggles. He wrote, "To have left one's possessions is nothing ; the great task is to watch over our hearts, which are full of obscure hesita-

tions." He went on to say that no doubt Severus
knew as well as he did how painful and dangerous
was the combat wherein our cowardice and sloth were
pitted against the service of God. He understood
better than when he lived in the world the nature of
concupiscence — the conflict of the flesh and the
spirit. What could be better for us than to cherish
within our souls the loving presence of Jesus Christ?
He would then uproot from the field of our hearts
the thorns and other noxious plants. Just as in laying the foundations of a house, we brought to light
all sorts of hidden things that had to be extirpated
— stones, roots of trees, serpents, nests of vipers —
so in exploring the depths of our hearts, in our effort
to set them free from the cares of this world, we discovered there the roots of our evil habits, and the
hiding-places built there by the enemies of our salvation. Such was actually his present misery. He
had found that to live according to faith much more
was necessary than merely to avoid sin, which was
to live according to the law. "So do not praise me
for what I have done, but pray that God will complete his work in me."

IV

It would be an entirely inadequate picture of Paulinus, if we represented him merely as a solitary, living
a life of retirement in his cell, given wholly to study
and prayer. He was rather an apostle, working for
the establishment on earth of the reign of justice and
charity. In his cell he gained inspiration and
spiritual power; but outside he carried on an active
apostolate through his teaching, by word of mouth
and by his letters. He had contact with large numbers of pilgrims, who flocked to Nola every year on
the Feast of Saint Felix. He himself made an an-
nual pilgrimage to Rome on the Feast of Saint Peter
and Saint Paul.

His influence was immensely extended when in
409 he was consecrated Bishop of Nola. It was at
a critical time, just after the city had been captured
by Alaric the Goth. Paulinus was then a true father
in God to a terrified population. He ransomed
many captives, and fed those who had been despoiled
of their possessions.

It is probable that Theresa lived long enough to
see him consecrated bishop, but died soon afterwards.
It would be interesting to know what were the defects in her character which prevented her being enrolled in the calendar of the saints. Her sacrifices

appeared to be quite as heroic as those made by Paulinus, and we know in what high esteem she was held by Saint Ambrose and Saint Augustine. It would be idle to speculate, as we know very little of her life after she settled in Nola.

After his consecration as bishop, Paulinus continued to live in his monastery, but visited frequently in his diocese and his flock became devoted to him. In the words of Cardinal Lépicier, "blessed are the people for whom Providence has procured the benefit of a pastor who is good, holy, learned, vigilant and loving as was Paulinus." He built an aqueduct for Nola, a basilica at Fondi, and another at Nola.

To the end of his life he displayed a rare genius for friendship, as we can see from his letters and poems. In the words of Monseigneur Baudrillart, one of his best modern biographers, "to instruct one another, to edify, to assist in the exercise of charity —such were in his eyes the true fruits of Christian friendship." Wace and Piercy in the *Dictionary of Christian Biography* [1] say that "his letters are generally clear and intelligible, pleasing as regards style ; remarkable for humility of mind, an affectionate disposition, and a cheerful playful humor, free from all moroseness or ascetic bitterness."

In the theological controversy between Saint

[1] P. 813.

Jerome and Saint Rufinus, both of whom were his friends, he refused to pronounce judgment. He was well acquainted with the heretic Pelagius, and did not seem quite so ready as Augustine to condemn him for his teachings. In many matters of theological speculation, where the faith was not involved, he preferred to suspend judgment. When Saint Augustine wrote him to ask his opinion about the manner of life of the disembodied spirits before the resurrection, and of their bodily existence after the resurrection, he replied that in his opinion it was more important to seek to know how to conduct ourselves in the present life, than to try to solve problems where our solutions could never attain to certainty.

The character of Saint Paulinus of Nola displays an unusual combination of gentleness and strength, humility and decisiveness, humanism and unworldliness, charity and self-discipline, activity and contemplation. It was as if the natural virtues, which he developed by being trained in the best traditions of paganism, were enriched and adorned by the supernatural virtues which the Holy Ghost infused into his soul after his conversion. What most endears him to us and makes the study of his life so bracing a tonic was his habitual capacity of taking by himself a decision and embracing it whole-heartedly. This

natural quality, ennobled and transfigured by his love
for Christ crucified, made him the saint whom we
love and venerate.

He has revealed to us something of his secret in
his poem, *The Word of the Cross :*

> Look on thy God, Christ hidden in our flesh.
> A bitter word, the Cross, and bitter sight :
> Hard rind without, to hold the heart of heaven,
> Yet sweet it is ; for God upon that tree
> Did offer up his life : upon that rood
> My life hung, that my life might stand in God.
> Christ, what am I to give thee for my life ?
> Unless take from thy hands the cup they hold,
> To cleanse me with the precious draught of death.
> What shall I do ?   My body to be burned ?
> Make myself vile ?   The debt's not paid out yet.
> Whate'er I do, it is but I and thou,
> And still do I come short, still must thou pay
> My debts, O Christ ; for debts thyself hadst none.
> What love may balance thine ?   My Lord was found
> In fashion like a slave, that so his slave
> Might find himself in fashion like his Lord.
> Think you the bargain's hard, to have exchanged
> The transient for the eternal, to have sold
> Earth to buy heaven ?   More dearly God bought me.[1]

[1] Translation by Helen Waddell, *Mediaeval Latin Lyrics*, p. 41.

SAINT MARGARET OF SCOTLAND
[1045-1083]

I

IF we accept the tradition of her birth in Hungary, Saint Margaret was of mixed blood. Through her father, Edward Aetheling, exiled heir to the English throne, she descended from a long line of Saxon kings. Through her mother, Agatha, a kinswoman of Saint Stephen of Hungary, she was in the line of the Roman Emperors.

Although no record has yet been found in Hungary of Edward's sojourn, there is a strong tradition that he fled there for safety, and that his children, Edgar, Christina and Margaret, were born there. Assuming the truth of this tradition, Margaret must have been influenced in her childhood by the religious atmosphere of Saint Stephen's Court. Although this saintly king had died, the enthusiasm of a newly converted people was still at a high pitch.

Edward the Confessor, having no heir, requested Prince Edward to bring his family to London, that when the time came he might succeed to the throne.

It must have been a keen disappointment to King Edward, that the Prince died soon after landing in England — especially as Edgar, his oldest son, had no capacities for kingship. Margaret, then a girl of twelve, received lasting impressions from association with her saintly great-uncle, the King. She watched with him the erection of the historic shrine which was to be his memorial, Westminster Abbey. It is possible that he suggested her future visit to Scotland and her betrothal to King Malcolm, whom he had helped in his struggle with the usurper Macbeth.

After the Norman Conquest, Edgar, with his sisters Christina and Margaret, and their mother, took refuge in Scotland. There is a romantic tale that they first set out for the Continent, but that a storm drove their ship to the coast of Scotland, where they were hospitably received by Malcolm ; and that as soon as he saw her, Malcolm fell in love with Margaret, who was then about twenty-one.

Malcolm asked Edgar for the hand of his sister, but Margaret hesitated. Like her sister Christina, who afterwards became an Abbess, she had yearnings for the religious life. We are told by her biographer Turgot that "when very young she had learned to despise worldly vanities, and to walk in the paths of virtue and truth." After much prayer, she concluded that the circumstances indicated that marriage was her vocation. As they were in the power of Malcolm, she really had no other choice.

As we read the conventional biographies of Saint Margaret, we are tempted to cast them aside as improbable, and to turn to the secular historians for a more sober verdict. Freeman, for example, would have no Catholic bias. His *Norman Conquest* would surely give us no rose-colored view of Saint Margaret. Then we come across this rhapsodical outburst about her marriage :[1]

It was indeed a good day for Malcolm and for Scotland when Margaret was persuaded or constrained to exchange the easy self-dedication of the cloister for the harder task of doing her duty in that state of life to which it had pleased God to call her. Margaret became the mirror of wives, mothers, and Queens, and none ever more worthily earned the honours of saintship. Her gentle influence reformed whatever needed to be reformed in her husband, and none laboured more diligently for the advance of all temporal and spiritual enlightenment in her adopted country.

They were married at Dunfermline, probably in 1068. Malcolm was a widower. The marriage was celebrated with barbaric pomp amid national rejoicings, and was of the utmost importance in its results for England. In the words of Freeman,[2]

[1] Vol. IV, p. 510.
[2] Vol. III, p. 12.

"It was through Margaret that the old kingly blood of England passed into the veins of the descendants of the Conqueror. The tree returns to the root when Henry I marries Matilda the daughter of Margaret ; it bears leaves at the birth of her children." Thus it happened that two years after England had become French through the Norman Conquest, Scotland became English through the marriage of Margaret with Malcolm.

II

MARGARET's first task was to civilize her husband. Malcolm was primarily a warrior, and he could neither read nor write. His ruthless raids into the north of England had spread havoc, and he dragged into captivity multitudes of fair-haired Saxons. The Queen sought to beautify his gloomy dwellings with rich tapestries, which she had brought with her from the South. She insisted on his being accompanied by suitable attendants when he sat in state or went out among his subjects. She bought gold and silver vessels for the royal table, and procured panes of glass for the windows of his castles in Edinburgh and Dunfermline.

She was able to mould him like wax in her hands. Yet he was intensely jealous of her and his suspicions sometimes made him ridiculous. In the forest of Dunfermline was a secret cave to which she often retired for prayer. An evil-minded courtier suggested to the King that she went there for no good purpose. The King resolved to see for himself what went on in this secret place, so one day he followed her stealthily at a distance. As he approached the cave he heard her voice in tones of entreaty. He seized his sword and was about to break through the bushes at the entrance to the cave when he caught her words more distinctly. She was praying for the conversion of his soul. Filled with remorse, he threw himself at her feet and begged to be forgiven.

Gradually he learned from her example how to pray, as he also learned to show mercy to the poor. The rough soldier repented of his sins and became so devout that his name is included in some Scottish Calendar among the saints. Sometimes he followed her into the dark church where together they would spend the night in prayer and vigil. Turgot tells how "there grew up in the King a sort of dread of offending one whose life was so venerable, for he could not but perceive from her conduct that Christ dwelt within her. Nay, more, he readily obeyed her wishes and prudent counsels in all things."

Though he could not read, he loved to handle her books of devotion. Often he would take one of them secretly to have it illuminated or ornamented with gold and precious stones. One of the most prized of these treasures was the Book of the Gospels, which the Queen took with her on her travels. One day the bearer carelessly let it slip from its wrappings into a river they were crossing. When it was finally discovered at the bottom of the stream, though its leaves were kept in motion by the current, the letters of gold were found unharmed. This was thought to be a miracle, but perhaps it was only a proof of the goldsmith's perfect art. This volume is still preserved in the Bodleian Library at Oxford.

III

In her married life of sixteen years, Margaret bore the King six sons and two daughters. It is significant of her dominating influence that English names were given to all these children : Edward, Ethelred, Edmund, Edgar, Alexander, David, Matilda and Mary. The mother herself instructed them in their younger years about Christ and their religious duties so far as their age would permit. We may judge as to the general tenor of their religious training from the following passage in the Douay Chronicle :

[81]

You will be curious to know what instruction this holy Queen left her children. Truly this curiosity is too reasonable to receive a repulse :

1. To die a thousand deaths rather than commit one mortal sin.

2. To give sovereign honor and absolute adoration to the Most Holy Trinity, and to have particular respect and veneration to the most Blessed Virgin, the Mother of God.

3. To be charitable to the poor, to protect orphans and relieve them in their necessities.

4. To abhor all obscene language and uncleanness.

5. To converse with persons of blameless lives and to follow their judgments and counsels.

6. To be firm, constant and unchangeable in maintenance of the Catholic Faith.

Though Margaret was a devoted mother, she never spoiled her children. We are told that "she charged the governor who had charge of the nursery to curb the children, to scold them, and to whip them whenever they were naughty, as frolicsome children will often be."

As they grew up, one of them went astray, but only for a time. The eldest, Edward, was killed in battle along with his father. Ethelred became lay Abbot of Dunkeld and Earl of Fife. Edmund, after a reckless wandering life, repented and became a monk. The three sons who succeeded to the throne were among the best kings Scotland ever had. Edgar the Peaceable was "a sweet and amiable man, like his kinsman the holy King Edward in every way." Alexander the Fierce was more like his father. The Chronicler says he was "a lettered and godly man, very humble and amiable towards the clerics and regulars, but terrible beyond measure toward the rest of his subjects; a man of large heart, exerting himself in all things beyond his strength." The greatest of Margaret's children was David, who received his mother's special blessing when as a little child he knelt beside her deathbed. He reigned for twenty-nine years, and is commonly regarded as one of the best and noblest of Scottish kings. "In his days he illumined his lands with kirks and with abbeys."

Matilda, who married Henry I of England, came to be known universally as the Good Queen Maud. On her tomb was written in golden letters: "A day would not suffice to tell of all her goodness and uprightness of character." She washed and kissed the feet of lepers. When asked whether her royal husband would approve of such actions, she replied: "I prefer the feet of the Eternal King before the lips of any mortal Prince." Mary became the wife of Count Eustace of Boulogne and the mother of Matilda, of whom was born Stephen, the English King.

IV

But to return to Margaret. She lost no time in persuading Malcolm to reform the abuses in his kingdom, in order that vice might be punished and virtue rewarded. She criticized the long delays in the courts of justice, and asked that the suits of the poor be given preference before all others. She urged him to soften the insolence of his soldiers and forbid their pillaging the homes of the Scottish people. She sought to banish incontinence and appease quarrels. She ransomed many of the Saxon slaves whom Malcolm had brought to Scotland. Above all she implored him to give positions of influence in the Church to priests who were eminent for their learning and virtue, that by rightly teaching the Faith and administering the Sacraments they might bring down the Divine blessing on the nation.

She took advantage of her influential position to reform abuses in the national Church. Certain lax practices and peculiar customs of the old Celtic Church had lingered on and kept the Church in Scotland out of harmony with the rest of the Catholic Church. The Queen wrote to Lanfranc, Archbishop of Canterbury, acquainting him with the state of the Church, and he sent Friar Goldwin and two monks to instruct her. As a result a council of bishops and other ecclesiastics and laymen was held, at which the King acted as interpreter, and the Queen defended the proposed changes. Marriage with one's step-mother or with a brother's widow was forbidden. The Lenten fast was to begin on Ash-Wednesday instead of the first Monday in Lent. Certain changes were made in the ritual of the Mass. Easter Communion was made obligatory. The practice was instituted of returning thanks after meals, which came to be known as Saint Margaret's Blessing. A reform which met with stubborn resistance was the one which made Sunday trading unlawful. But Margaret supported her case so strongly with arguments drawn from Holy Scripture and the Fathers that all opposition was silenced.

In the discussion on Easter Communion, when she asked the laity to explain their neglect of this practice, they replied : "The Apostle, when speaking of persons who eat and drink unworthily, says that they eat and drink judgment to themselves. Now, since we admit that we are sinners, we fear to approach that mystery lest we should eat and drink judgment to ourselves."

"What !" exclaimed the Queen, "shall no one who is a sinner taste that holy mystery ? If so, then it follows that no one at all should receive it, for no one is free from sin, no, not even the infant whose life is but one day upon the earth. And if no one ought to receive it, why did Our Lord make this pronouncement in the Gospel, 'except you eat the flesh of the Son of Man and drink His blood, you shall not have life in you'? It is the man who, without confession or penance, but carrying there with him the defilements of his sins, presumes to approach the Sacred Mysteries, such an one I say it is who eats and drinks judgment to himself. Whereas we who, many days previously, have made confession of our sins and have been cleansed from their stains by chastening penance, by trying fasts, by almsgiving and tears, approaching in the Catholic Faith to the Lord's table on the day of His resurrection, receive the body and blood of Jesus Christ, the immaculate Lamb, not to judgment but to the remission of our sins and as a health-giving preparation for eternal happiness."

She built a church at Dunfermline in memory of her marriage, dedicating it to the Blessed Trinity for a three-fold end: the redemption of her husband's soul, the welfare of her own, and the salvation of their children. She rebuilt and restored the monastery at Iona, which had sent forth so many missionaries for the conversion of Scotland, and had been the burial-place of her kings. She provided vestments for many churches, and chalices and other vessels of gold and silver which she had brought from England and Hungary. She established a workshop in her palace where many women were trained in the making of ecclesiastical vestments. "Copes for the cantors, chasubles, stoles, altarcloths, and other priestly vestments and church ornaments were always to be seen, either already made of an admirable beauty, or in the course of preparation."

v

THROUGH her constant faithfulness in prayer, Queen Margaret brought down God's blessings bountifully upon her family and the nation. Through her severe self-discipline — she fasted forty days before Christmas as well as in Lent — she kept herself humble, and thus allowed God to work through her His mighty works.

The story of her spiritual life, told in Latin by her confessor Turgot, has been translated by W. Forbes-Leith, S.J. Turgot tells how she often besought him to rebuke her faults, and sometimes chided him for "being drowsy" in his duty. She knew the dangers of flattery for those in her position, and quoted to him the verse of the Psalm: "The just man shall correct me in mercy and shall reprove me ; but let not the oil of the sinner fatten my head."

In spite of her spotless life, she kept ever before her the idea of judgment. She meditated frequently on the words of the Apostle James: "What is our life? It is a vapor which appeareth for a little while and afterwards shall vanish away." Turgot declares that the strictness of her austerities brought upon her a severe infirmity. Her nights were often spent in prayer. "She began, continued and ended nothing without prayer." "In church no one was so silent and composed as she, no one so rapt in prayer." She recited the Breviary daily. She would often attend five or six Masses, and then before she partook of her frugal meal would wait on twenty-four poor people whom she entirely supported.

Her days of ceaseless toil, her nights of prayer and her strict self-discipline, undoubtedly brought on her early death. She predicted that her end was near. Some time before her death, she was compelled to part with Turgot as her confessor, he having been appointed Prior of Durham. Before saying good-bye to him she made to him a general confession of her whole life, and then addressed him thus: "I now bid you farewell, I shall not continue much longer in this world, but you will live after me for a considerable time. There are two things which I beg of you. One is that as long as you survive me you will remember me in your prayers. The other is that you will take some care about my sons and daughters. Lavish your affection upon them. Teach them above all things to love and fear God." He adds, "I bade the queen my last farewell, for after that day I never saw her face in the flesh."

Her strength failed gradually. For the last six months of her life she was confined to her bed. Against her warnings and pleadings, Malcolm insisted on going forth to battle on the Northumberland border. William Rufus had broken faith with him, and he felt the honor of Scotland was at stake. Prince Edward and Prince Edgar accompanied the King. The anxious days dragged on, and no tidings came.

One day — the day on which the King and Prince Edward were slain — Margaret said to her confessor, "Perhaps on this very day such a heavy calamity may befall the realm of Scotland as has not been for many ages past." Knowing that her end was near, she received the Last Sacraments.

Finally a weary, mud-stained messenger appeared in her chamber. It was Prince Edgar. He was overwhelmed to find his mother at the point of death.

She roused herself enough to ask him, "How are the king and my Edward?"

He answered, "They are well."

"I know it, my boy, I know it," she sighed, "but by this holy Cross and by the bond of our common blood, I adjure you to tell me the truth."

Then he told her that both his father and his brother had met their deaths in battle. Raising her eyes toward heaven, she exclaimed: "I give praise and thanks to Thee, Almighty God, for that Thou hast willed that I should endure such deep sorrow at my departing, and I trust that by means of this suffering it is Thy pleasure that I should be cleansed from some of the stains of my sins."

Thereupon, knowing that her death was at hand, she began the prayer before the priest's Communion in the Mass:

"O Lord Jesus Christ, who by the will of the Father and the co-operation of the Holy Ghost, didst by Thy death give life to the world, deliver me" — and as she uttered the words, "deliver me," God answered her prayer and set her soul free from the body.

SAINT ELIZABETH OF HUNGARY
[1207-1231]

In narrating the life of a saint, one is tempted to color the facts to suit one's own conceptions of sanctity; to omit disquieting features which are difficult to explain; and to place the emphasis where one thinks it should be placed rather than where it was placed by the Almighty God.

A saint is a masterpiece of God — therefore in some sense a revelation of the mind and will of the divine Artist. In every saint we may discern one or more characteristics of the life of Our Lord. If we no longer possessed the authentic records which we have in the *Gospels*, we might piece together from the lives of the saints in every age a composite picture of Christ, which would not differ essentially from that portrayed in the *New Testament*.

The dominant characteristic in the life of Elizabeth of Hungary was the desire to surrender herself utterly in an all-absorbing love. We see in her a faithful imitation or rather reproduction of the human love of Christ, as in the poor man of Assisi we contemplate his poverty.

I

THE daughter of the King of Hungary, Elizabeth was sent in her fourth year to the Wartburg in Thuringia to be educated as the future bride of Ludwig, Count of Thuringia and Hesse, to whom she had been promised by her parents. He was seven years older than she, but they were brought up together; and their childish friendship developed into the strongest affection of Elizabeth's life.

Elizabeth's mother was assassinated two years after the child had arrived at the Wartburg. Soon afterwards Ludwig's elder brother Herman and also his father died, the latter from a violent death. Suffering and sympathy bound Elizabeth more closely to Ludwig, and also gave her a deeper sense of spiritual need.

It has been said that in the lives of all predestined souls there is a particular moment when they experience the feeling that Jesus is personally pursuing them, that He wants them all for Himself and that He expects a something of them. This personal encounter with Christ is decisive; it changes the whole subsequent course of their lives.

This moment came to Elizabeth as she was walking from the Wartburg to Eisenach. She met a beggar on the path and it seemed to her that the man

[92]

looked like Jesus. She ministered to the man's needs, and from that moment felt that her vocation was to clothe the naked and to feed the hungry.

Henceforth her daily habits were altered. She visited the poor in their homes, talked with them, touched them, and often brought them home with her to the castle. One day she happened upon a sick beggar with a repulsive disease of the scalp. She led him to a secret room in the castle; and later her servants found her with the man's head on her knees; she was cutting his hair, washing and perfuming it! The servants were shocked, but she only laughed.

On another occasion, when seeking to revive a poor man who was starving, she tried with her own hands to milk a cow. The animal, however, refused to be milked.

Elizabeth received no encouragement from Ludwig's mother or the other members of the household, but only cold looks and reproaches. They felt that her precocious piety and charity might be suitable in a nun, but were hardly befitting the fiancée of the future Count of Thuringia.

She was married to Ludwig when she was fourteen and he twenty-one. He would not listen to the slanders of the court of Eisenach against her. Though he was never canonized by the Church, yet in popular estimation he has been regarded as a saint.

[93]

He accorded his bride perfect liberty to practice alms-giving and make her visits of mercy as she chose ; and placed abundance of means at her disposal. He also allowed her to observe the special dietary rules she had laid upon herself.

Saint Francis of Assisi died only six years after their marriage, and the first Franciscan friars had already arrived at Eisenach. Elizabeth watched one of them, Brother Roger, as he begged his food from house to house, with gaiety and good spirits in a snow-storm on a cold winter day. Afterwards she talked with him and he spoke to her of Francis, and how Christ had taught him to imitate not merely his poverty, but his being stripped of his garments and nailed to the cross. This meeting with the Friar Roger took place shortly after her marriage and there can be little doubt that the Friar urged her to seek release from her marriage vows and to renounce everything, so as to be free to serve Christ.

That Elizabeth did not take this step was probably due to the restraining influence of her confessor. Ludwig had written to the Pope, Gregory IX, requesting him to appoint a director who might guide the countess in the way of conformity to God's will and temper the excesses of her fiery nature. In response the Holy Father designated a man who was full of zeal for the Church, a secular priest, the inquisitor Conrad of Marburg.

Elizabeth submitted humbly to Conrad's direction and found in him a priest coldly prudent, with an inflexible will. He was austere, incorruptible, uncompromising even to brutality, a reformer by nature; fully conscious, however, of the value of the soul committed to him and of his responsibilities. He endeavored to moderate her ambition to be a mendicant and to lessen the generosity of her charities. Instead he induced her to make sacrifices of some of her personal gifts and inclinations. He began by demanding of her not only docility but absolute surrender to his direction. Accordingly she took, in the presence of her mother-in-law and children, a solemn vow of obedience to Conrad in everything save what concerned the rights of her husband in the married state.

Elizabeth's love for her husband was the natural fruit of the pure friendship which began in their childhood. Even after their marriage, they addressed each other as "dear brother" and "dear sister." It was not, however, what one might call a purely spiritual love. Those who regard that sort of love as a necessary adjunct of sanctity should read an account of their married life. They were passionately devoted to each other. No romance could be more touching. She could scarcely bear being parted from him when he went away on a journey or on a military expedition ; to serve the Emperor or to make a visit to Rome. To quote from Ida Condenhove's study of the Saint :

Then she cannot be parted from him, follows him for days in all weathers ; puts on widow's weeds. So passionately does she cling to the sight of the beloved, so much does she hunger for him, so deeply even to the heart's core does she know, does she feel, the bliss of remaining for work or rest, in the warm, living presence of a beloved being. And boundless is the passion of her joy, her starved longing for his tenderness, when he returns — impetuously, heedless of his retinue, she throws herself into his arms and cannot let go of him, so insatiable is her joy at the sight of him.[1]

Elizabeth was fully aware of the dangers to her faith in so absorbing an affection. She knew that God must come first in her life if he was to be in it at all ; that her husband and children were to be loved in God and for his sake, rather than as ends in themselves. She had the wisdom to see that her prayer life was the fortress which must be kept impregnable against all invasions from the world.

According to some of the mediaeval biographers,

[1] *The Nature of Sanctity*, by Ida Condenhove, p. 22. Sheed & Ward, 1932.

the possibility that her passionate love for her husband might make her forget God was impressed upon her mind one day at Mass. She found herself gazing admiringly at her husband, who was attired in festal array. She forgot where she was, until the bell rang for the consecration. She glanced at the altar just as the priest was elevating the host, and perceived that it was bleeding! Overwhelmed with remorse, she lingered long in the Church weeping and disconsolate over the sign that had been given her. Ludwig tried in vain to comfort her.

Ludwig, a true son of that age of faith, volunteered for the crusade planned by Frederick II. When he first took the cross, he did not wear it on his shoulder, "that his dear hostess, Elizabeth, be not aware of it and be distressed and frightened thereby, she loving him beyond measure and with her whole heart."

It was by accident that she made the discovery. She was playing one day with the sword-belt of the young Landgraf and something slipped out of the pocket. It was a piece of black cloth marked with a cross. At once she understood. Of all the sweet joys of her life, God had chosen this supreme joy to be signed with the cross of sacrifice! Ludwig admitted that he had enlisted for the crusade. He too had heard the appeal of Christ and had taken the

vow to fight for the recovery of the Holy places
from the infidel.

Ludwig was firm despite his wife's tears and prot-
estations. Though she was with child and in great
pain and grief, she rode for a day with him long after
his mother and relatives had returned to the castle.
Even then she could not part with him, knowing that
it might easily be her last sight of him on earth. She
rode with him another day, until finally his knights
had almost to force him to send her home. On her
return she mourned like a widow and remained a
long time alone in grief and prayer.

Elizabeth bore her husband three children : Herman, Sophia, and Gertrude. Herman was only
five, when Ludwig set out for the Holy Land.
When she brought her third child into the world, she
was unable to get word to her husband. Finally the
terrible news was brought by his mother that Ludwig
had died of a fever in Brindisi before sailing from
Italy.

II

IT would be an error to say that Elizabeth lived
wholly for her husband while he was alive and, only
when he was taken from her, devoted herself to the
service of the poor. Just as Ludwig had many concerns of his own in which his wife had no share —

military expeditions, journeys with the Emperor, the supervision of his estates — so Elizabeth had her hospital at Eisenach to look after and hundreds of poor families to feed. When her husband was away on business of state, she spent all her time in these good works. Even when he was at home, she maintained this wise division of interests.

Soon after the death of Ludwig, Elizabeth forsook the Wartburg. There is evidence that she was driven out. The cause of her departure is not certain. In any event Henry and Conrad, the brothers of Ludwig, having assumed charge of the government of Thuringia, ruthlessly took possession of the castle. They were not too friendly with Elizabeth and for a time withheld from her the heritage which was hers by right.

Another reason for her leaving was hinted at by one of her servants, Irmingard, in her deposition in the process of canonization. She testified that Master Conrad, Elizabeth's director, because of his scrupulous zeal for justice and the welfare of the poor, had for some time forbidden her to eat or make use of anything which she did not certainly know had been produced without injustice. For this reason Ludwig had permitted her at his table to observe a particular rule of diet. After his death, inasmuch as she was deprived of her heritage, she could remain no longer at the Wartburg without violating her conscience and the orders of her confessor.

She fled from the castle in the night and walked through the streets of Eisenach in the rain seeking for shelter. She found a shed which had formerly been a hog-pen and there passed the rest of the night. She felt exhilarated by her new-found freedom ; and it seemed as if her love of poverty had at last found satisfaction. When the bell of the Friars Minor sounded for matins she went to their church and asked them to chant the *Te Deum*.

During the months that followed, her distress was somewhat alleviated. She was invited with her children to share the hospitality of an aunt who was an abbess. Soon afterwards she received an offer of marriage from the half-pagan philosopher and Emperor Frederick II. The crown of empress, however, had no allurements for her and she declined his offer.

The returning crusaders brought back the body of her husband and reproached his brother, Henry, for withholding the fief and dowry which were her due. He made over to her a considerable sum of money and the little town of Marburg. She used the money to found at Marburg a hospital where with her companions, Guda and Ysentrude, she ministered with her own hands to the sick poor. She donned the habit of a Franciscan tertiary. It was on a Good Friday that she laid her hands on the bare altar of the Minorite church at Marburg, and Brother Bruckardt cut off her hair and put the rope girdle upon her.

Her associates and her confessor have testified to the many heroic acts of virtue which she performed in that hospital. There was a little boy with only one eye and paralysed, whom she waited on five or six times during the night, washing his clothes with her own hands, telling him while she nursed him all sorts of amusing stories. When he died she became the nurse of a leprous girl, until her confessor, Conrad, heard of it and ordered the child removed. When Conrad had gone away to preach, she took care of a scrofulous child who had lost all his hair and treated him with ointments made from recipes "learned from whom I know not," wrote Conrad to the Pope. This afflicted boy was seated in a chair next to Elizabeth's bed when he died.

Christian charity for her was not simply philanthropy — an enterprise of doing good to the unfortunate; it bore the wounds of the love of Christ and conformed itself to the special conditions of life with him. The love of Christ for her implied the love of his cross and the bearing of it after him. All whom Christ loved were her friends. She saw in the poor, the sick, the maimed, and the blind, the same qualities and possibilities that her Lord saw in them and that is why she loved them.

Psychologists have advanced various ingenious theories to explain what they regard as the fanatical asceticism of Elizabeth. One theory is that after the death of her husband she had to find an outlet for her emotional nature, lest she be consumed with grief. She chose this work among the poor because it would take her far from the associations and memories of her happy life with Ludwig.

Another theory is that throughout her life she sought humiliation and self-abasement. She knew that only the practice of such virtues could save her from the racial curse of the "will to power" which she had inherited from her father, King Andrew of Hungary, and her mother, Gertrude of Meranien. Both families shared a tradition of ambition and violence. When her mother was cruelly murdered, Elizabeth learnt in childhood the tragic consequences of this lust for power; and under the influence of divine grace she resolved to root out from her own soul this dark inheritance.

This latter theory has been skilfully developed by Maria Marsch, the Viennese Catholic biographer of Elizabeth. She says:

She wanted to heal and make compensation for one extreme by another, to quench the burning lust for power and possessions, so deep-rooted in her family, by abasement and self-denial, so deep and so unbounded that she bore even the blows of Conrad of Marburg. That is the creative idea which informed Elizabeth's life.[1]

These theories seem too complicated to suit the simplicity and continuity of Elizabeth's character. She was very young when she died and apparently never lost her child-like heart. She never seems to have gone through that inner upheaval known as conversion. She belonged to the class known as the "once-born."

From early childhood she professed a whole-hearted devotion to Christ and his poor. Her works of charity were indeed more numerous during the lifetime of her husband than after his death. Penance and self-denial were clearly developed traits even when she was a young girl, according to the testimony of her playmates. When she became a bride she disciplined her body by fasting and scourging and made her servants chastise her on Fridays and fast days. Though she arrayed herself in purple and gold to please her husband and his court, yet underneath these costly robes she wore a hair-shirt. When her husband was away she put on

---

[1] Quoted in *The Nature of Sanctity*, p. 47.

humble garments and sat with her maids to spin wool.

One day early in her married life she confided to Ludwig her fantastic idea that it would be pleasant if they were living together as poor peasants — like so many in his dominions — he following the oxen with the plough and she milking the cows; and if he possessed only a "yoke" of land and two hundred sheep. He laughed aloud and agreed that it would indeed be splendid poverty if he had two hundred sheep!

When he returned from doing court duty at Cremona and his stewards complained to him that his wife by her indiscriminate almsgiving during his absence had wasted his possessions, he made the reply: "Let her give in God's name and do good to the poor — as long as we keep the Wartburg and Neuenburg!"

There was apparently no cataclysmic change in Elizabeth's character or manner of life after her husband's death; nor have we any proof that, in order to counteract inherited tendencies and family traditions, she lived a life of calculated abasements and asceticism.

III

THE fact that Christ Our Lord singled out Elizabeth of Hungary for special attention and love does not mean that this world suddenly became for her a bed of roses. Incidentally there is too much talk about roses in connection with her. The famous story of the basket of food which she was taking to the poor, which was transformed into a basket of roses when she met her husband on the way and uncovered it at his request, is not authentic. If such a thing ever happened it was in connection with her great-niece, Saint Elizabeth of Portugal.

We learn more of the true character of Elizabeth of Hungary from her refusal to wear her jewelled coronet when she entered a church. To her it did not seem fitting that she should wear a crown of gold in the presence of Him who had worn a crown of thorns. So great was her love for Christ that she longed to suffer as he had suffered. Hence her life of self-denial, poverty, sacrifice and penance. She determined to imitate as far as possible His poverty, homelessness, fasting ; His nights of lonely prayer ; His agony in the garden ; the shame, the humiliations and torments of His Passion.

It was this soul, who earnestly desired perfection, who sought to find her life by losing it for the sake of Christ, and to gain a treasure in heaven by selling all that she had and giving the money to the poor — that by order of the Pope was committed to the spiritual direction of Master Conrad. We may not approve of the methods of this coldly reasonable director, but we must admit that he produced notable results. "By their fruits you shall know them."

Under Conrad's severe direction, however, Elizabeth did not lose her spontaneity or her mischievous inclination to act contrary to her confessor's orders when his back was turned. He had forbidden her to give alms of more than a penny. She obeyed, but told the beggars to come back and take as much as they wished. It appears also from Conrad's letter to Pope Gregory IX that Elizabeth came to Marburg against his counsel.

Conrad was fully conscious of the immense responsibility involved in the direction of such a soul ; and it could not have been an easy task to hold in check so ardent and impulsive a young woman who acted first and reflected afterwards. She had been powerfully attracted by the personality and example of the young Franciscan Brother Roger, and would gladly have sacrificed her family wealth to become a wandering beggar. Conrad ruled otherwise.

We have seen how she loved the children of the poor, the undernourished, the maimed and those stricken with loathsome diseases. When she first left the Wartburg she separated herself temporarily from her children in order that they might not know the misery of their mother. At Marburg, according to the deposition of Ysentrude, she asked of God three things : first, that he would give her the contempt of all things temporal, second, that he would take away from her the love of children, and third, that he would inspire her with courage to despise insults.

Her two oldest children, Henry and Sophia, were taken to Kreuzburg. The youngest, Gertrude, in pursuance of an understanding with Ludwig before he went on the Crusade, was entrusted to the care of the Premonstratensian Sisters of Altenburg. Their future in this world did not seem to be compromised. Henry died in his nineteenth year ; Sophia married the Duke of Brabant, Henry II, and lived to the age of sixty ; Gertrude became the Abbess of Altenburg and is now venerated as Blessed.

It was plainly the teaching of Our Lord that we must be in such a disposition of soul as to be willing to renounce and part with everything, however near and dear it may be to us, that would keep us from following him. That is the meaning of Our Lord's hard saying about "hating" father, mother, wife, children and so forth (Saint Luke, xIV, 26, see foot-note in Douai version). When Saint Peter said to Our Lord, "Behold we have left all things and followed Thee," he replied, "Amen I say to you, there is no man that has left home or parents or brethren or wife or children for the Kingdom of God's sake who shall not receive much more in this present time, and in the world to come life everlasting . . ."

At last Elizabeth reached the state of utter destitution and abandonment; nothing further remained of which she might be deprived — so she must have felt! Master Conrad knew better, and gave orders that her faithful servants — Guda and Ysentrude — who had been her companions and playmates from her earliest years at the Wartburg and were now the best friends she had, should be sent away from her. In their place he designated as her assistants in her works of charity a lay brother, a pious but unattractive young woman, and a widow of noble birth but of harsh and irritable manner.

Even Guda and Ysentrude defended Conrad. They said he meant well, because "he feared that the sight of the two faithful women who followed her from Wartburg and shared her penury might fill her with pain and longing for her former life. So he took them away 'because of the temptation'." [1]

Of all the material joys, bodily comforts and human relationships which had constituted her life in this world, nothing remained: father, mother, husband, wealth, position, prestige, children, friends — all were gone and she only in her twenty-fourth year.

[1] *The Nature of Sanctity*, p. 111.

Yet it could not be said that she was left desolate. Neither could she be said to be alone. Her throbbing heart was empty save for the devouring fire of her love for Jesus and the least of his brethren. She still had the companionship of Him who is altogether lovely, the fairest of the sons of men. She had refused the crown of an empress to be the handmaid of the King of Kings and Lord of Lords.

In her twenty-fourth year, on November 17, 1231, the Lord called her to the joys of the beatific vision. She was venerated immediately after her death, and canonized by Gregory IX in 1253.

SAINT LOUIS OF FRANCE
[1214-1270]

I<small>F</small> <small>IT</small> be true—as the modern saying goes—that
it is not how *long* we live, but how *much*, that mat-
ters, then Louis IX of France was a master in the
art of living.   He was the typical king of the greatest century of the Middle Ages, a peacemaker among
the nations, a crusader to the Holy Land, idolized
by the French people, respected by the Saracens.
He established justice, peace and prosperity in
France, and raised her to a place of pre-eminence in
Christendom.   In his private life he was happily
married and the father of eleven children ; he was
feared by the nobles and loved by the poor ; he
practised his religion humbly and by his invincible
faith and unceasing prayer maintained an unbroken
contact with God and the powers of the supernatural
world.   He wore his earthly crown without reproach,
and thereby gained a heavenly crown whose glory
will never fade.

I

THE first fact in the life of Saint Louis of France that rivets our attention is that he had a holy and capable mother, Blanche of Castile. She combined a genius for statesmanship with the best qualities of motherhood. Louis was her oldest son, and through the untimely death of his father, Louis VIII, became heir-presumptive to the throne when a boy of twelve. Blanche ruled the kingdom as regent with wisdom and vigor until he could be crowned as Louis IX. She repeatedly frustrated the plots of the feudal aristocracy against her son ; and went to war against the nobles when it was necessary in order to preserve the unity of the kingdom. She was more than a match for them and finally succeeded in making them respect the authority of the crown.

Blanche took Louis with her on her military campaigns, and had him sit beside her in the councils of state. This gave him training in the art of ruling, for he learned not only through precept, but through ocular demonstration. Blanche was not content to train her son to be a king ; she schooled him also in the ways of sanctity. She taught him the elements of Catholic faith and devotion, and drilled him in habits of prayer which he never abandoned.

From his earliest years she strove to impress upon his sensitive mind the value of holiness. She often said to him, "I would rather see you dead than know that you should live to commit a mortal sin."

When Louis was nineteen years of age, his mother decided that it was time for him to marry. She chose for him a child of twelve, the Princess Marguerite, the eldest daughter of Raymond Bérenger, Count of Provence. Perhaps she did not realize how beautiful the young princess was; later she apparently became jealous of her son's devotion to his wife. Perhaps Louis was surprised to find that his mother had chosen so pretty and graceful a girl to be his wife, but there is no evidence that he was displeased. Marguerite bore her husband eleven children.

Saint Francis de Sales, in the chapter on "Counsels for Married Persons," in his *Introduction to the Devout Life*, appeals to the example of this French royal saint as an illustration of the proper use to be made of mutual caresses in married life: "The great St. Louis, who was as rigorous towards his own flesh as he was tender in his love of his wife, was almost blamed for being lavish in such caresses, although in truth he rather deserved praise for knowing how to lay aside his martial and courageous spirit, and give these little demonstrations of affection; for although these little demonstrations of pure and frank affection do not bind hearts together, yet they bring them close together, and serve as a pleasant aid to mutual intercourse."

Throughout their married life, Louis never entered upon any serious undertaking without first gaining the permission of his wife. Father R. P. Surin, of the Society of Jesus, writing in 1652, praises this habit of the French king as exemplifying the quality of wisdom in conjugal love: "It is reported of St. Louis that he never disposed of his person without taking the advice of Madame Marguerite of Provence, his wife; and that when in captivity in the Holy Land, when he was treating of his ransom, before giving his final word, he demanded the privilege of speaking to the queen, who had accompanied him in the voyage to the Levant. Upon the infidels expressing their surprise, he replied that he could conclude nothing without her, *because she was his Lady,* and as such he owed her this respect. To act and speak in that way proved the wise love of the holy king for the queen his wife."

Once, however, Queen Marguerite refused the consent for which the king had asked. When their eldest son had reached the age when he might succeed to the throne, Louis told the queen secretly of his own desire to renounce the throne and become a

[113]

religious, and asked her to acquiesce in his pious intention. She shook her head and stamped her foot, and quickly put forward convincing arguments why he should remain king as long as he lived. He allowed himself to be persuaded, and never again brought up the subject.

The persistent jealousy which Blanche of Castile displayed towards the queen on many occasions proves that she was not a saint — as yet. Joinville, in his *Memoirs*, bears witness to this jealousy : "The harshness which Queen Blanche showed to Queen Marguerite was such that Queen Blanche would not allow her son to remain in his wife's company, if she could prevent it, except in the evening when he retired with her."

It is possible that Queen Blanche had a theory that a husband and wife might see too much of each other. However, King Louis and his wife so arranged matters that they could see each other when they wished on a winding staircase which connected their two rooms, by instructing their attendants to give them a signal when the queen mother came to either room, so that she always found either the king or the queen alone.

Joinville records that "once the king was with his wife, and she was in danger of death, being ill after the birth of a child. The Queen Blanche came there, took her son by the hand and said, 'Come away, you have no business here.' When Queen Marguerite saw that the mother was leading the king away, she cried out : 'Alas ! You will not let me see my lord either in life or death'; and then she swooned, and they thought she was dead. The king, who thought she was dying, returned, and it was with great trouble that she was brought to herself again."

The Sire de Joinville may not have been an entirely trustworthy authority on the relative merits of these two ladies. He was obviously a devoted partisan of Queen Marguerite ; he also sympathized with the feudal aristocratic party which Queen Blanche had fought and outwitted, and thus was prejudiced against her.

Marguerite intimated once or twice to Joinville that just because she was the wife of a saint she must not be considered, from a worldly standpoint, to be necessarily the happiest of women. Indeed she was not called upon to bear testimony to his sanctity in the process of canonization. Thirty-eight witnesses were called, but not the queen.

She often said of the king, *Il est si divers* — which translated into our language would probably be, "He is so queer !" For instance, when they were returning from Palestine, and the royal ship was in danger of being shipwrecked in a storm near the coasts of Cyprus, Joinville urged her to make a vow of a pilgrimage if they arrived safely in France.

She replied, "Sire, I would gladly make this vow ; but if the king learned that I had made it without consulting him, he would never permit me to fulfil the pilgrimage. The king is so queer !"

From the wifely point of view, the king was undoubtedly difficult to manage. The queen once expressed to him her vexation at his simple way of dressing and his lack of royal dignity.

"Madame," he asked, "would you be pleased if I covered myself with costly garments ?"

"I certainly would," she replied, "and I want you to do so."

"Well, I agree," said the king, "and am ready to please you, for the law of marriage requires that the husband should seek to please his wife. Only this obligation is reciprocal ; you will, therefore, be obliged to conform to my wish."

"And what is that wish ?" she demanded.

"It is that you should wear the most humble costume ; you will take mine, and I yours."

The queen would not consent to make the exchange, so she curtsied and left the room.

Louis IX of France is one of the most attractive saints just because he was a king. He used to the full the grace which God gave him, and thus made his royal dignity the instrument for the development of sanctity. There is no position in life, however exalted, that may not be so used. As Bourdaloue said in his sermon on the Feast of Saint Louis, "It is a sentiment very injurious to Providence to suppose that there are in the world any conditions absolutely opposed to saintliness; or that saintliness is in itself incompatible with certain conditions and states of which it is nevertheless admitted that God is the author."

Saint Louis manifested a fervent zeal for God, joined with a profound humility. He exemplified M. Henri Joly's definition of a saint as "the man who serves God heroically and out of love." He rose at midnight and summoned his clerks and chaplains to chant the Matins of the day and those of Our Lady. After a short interval, barely long enough to fall asleep, they were called to chant Prime. He heard each day a Mass for the dead, in addition to the Mass for the day, which was always sung. During Lent he heard three Masses a day, the last of which was said towards noon. When travelling on horseback, he caused his chaplains to sing as they rode the hours of Terce, Sext and None.

The carrying of the Cross into the Holy Land was impressed as an inescapable duty upon the mind of Saint Louis, when he was miraculously restored to health from a severe illness that followed his exhausting campaign in Guyenne in 1244. The whole nation was alarmed and rallied to the help of the sick king by prayers, alms and solemn processions. His mother prayed night and day with fastings and other austerities. She ordered the relics of the true Cross, the Crown of Thorns, and the Sacred Lance to be brought to the sick chamber that the king might touch them.

Finally the king awoke, as if from the sleep of death, and said feebly, "The grace of God has visited me from on high, and has recalled me from the dead." When he had completely regained his senses, he sent for the Bishop of Paris.

Upon his arrival with the Bishop of Meaux, the king astonished all by saying, "My Lord Bishop, I beg you to place the cross of foreign pilgrimage upon my shoulder."

The two bishops and both queens pleaded with him to wait until he had fully recovered his normal strength ; but he protested that he would take no food until he had received the cross. The bishop regretfully complied with his request.

Ever since Pope Urban II had in 1095 made the Crusade a work of piety, devout kings and princes had looked upon it, not as a war of aggression against the infidels, but as continuing the necessary defence of Europe and Christian civilization against pagan barbarism and the Moslem invasions. It was but carrying on the work begun with such energy by Charles Martel and Charlemagne. Saint Louis had seen the Tartar hordes, which had ravaged Poland, Silesia, Southern Russia, Moldavia and Hungary with fire and sword, appearing in 1240 on the frontiers of Germany. He hoped that an expedition into the Holy Land and the founding of a Christian kingdom of Jerusalem, might keep the Saracens from following in the wake of the barbarian invaders of Europe from the north and east. To wrest the Holy Land from the Turks did not seem to Saint Louis the fantastic adventure that it seems to many today.

Brother Salimbene, an Italian religious who was present at the provincial chapter of the minor friars at Sens, when the French king stopped on his way to the Crusade to ask for their prayers, has thus described Saint Louis as he appeared at that time:

"The king was weak, slight and thin, of a fair

height, with an angelic air, and a countenance full of grace. He came to the church of the minor friars, not with royal pomp, but in a pilgrim's habit, bearing on his neck his wallet and bread-bag, which marvellously adorned his royal shoulders."

Judged from a human standpoint, this Crusade of Saint Louis was a failure, not because he did not make adequate military preparations, but because a lack of coördination in the crusading forces of the various leaders resulted in disastrous delays in the invasion of Egypt. This gave the Saracens time to recover from their panic. Better, however, than any military success was the heroic refusal of the French king to save himself from capture by boarding his ship and thus deserting the main body of his soldiers who had already landed. They were all taken prisoners by the Saracens, and Saint Louis spent the next four years in captivity in the Holy Land. He finally paid a generous ransom, without haggling, for the release of himself and his army. Throughout the four years he did not cease to labor for the conversion of the Turks.

III

Saint Louis, as we have seen, loved his wife with a true and pure affection; he also took pains that his children should receive the best possible education. He often instructed them himself, and personally selected their teachers and masters.

According to Joinville, "Before he lay down in his bed, he made his children come round him and told them the deeds of good kings and emperors, and that they should take example by such good men. And he also told them the deeds of bad princes who, by their luxury, rapine and avarice, had lost their kingdoms. 'And I remind you of these things,' said he, 'that you may avoid them, so that God be not wroth against you.' He made them learn the hours of our Lady, and made them say the daily hours before him, to accustom them to hear the hours when they should govern their lands."

According to worldly standards, the children turned out creditably to their parents, though four of them died in youth. The eldest son, Louis, was a boy of high promise and probably the favorite of his father ; but he died in his sixteenth year, while the king was lying seriously ill at Fontainebleau.

Thinking his own death was near, the father wrote this last message to his son : "Fair son, I pray you to make the people of your kingdom love you ; for truly, I would rather a Scotchman came from Scotland to govern the people of the kingdom well and loyally than that you should govern them badly in the sight of all." The succession passed to Prince Philip, who became known as Philip the Bold.

Saint Louis ministered to countless numbers of the sick and needy, and with his own hands buried the bodies of many of his soldiers who died on the Crusade. At the royal table he fed numerous poor people daily with his own hands ; on Maundy Thursday he washed the feet of the poor and the lepers.

To love God and one's neighbor does not make one a saint, unless one also practises self-discipline. Probably the kinds of mortification practised by Saint Louis would not be widely popular today. He afflicted his body with a hair-shirt and frequent fasting ; he used the discipline and slept under sackcloth on ashes. His confessor finally made him give up the use of the hair-shirt, and forbade him to practise such extreme fasting as would unfit him for his royal duties. No doubt he found other more secret means of mortification. An intense personal love for their Saviour has ever made the saints eager to suffer for and along with Christ. As Saint Paul said, "If we suffer with him, we shall also reign with him."

IV

Not only does Louis IX of France occupy a high place among the saints because he was a king ; but he was one of the most loved of the kings of the Middle Ages because he was a saint.

The fundamental principles of his royal policy were justice to all classes and peace with all nations. When war became necessary as a defence against injustice, he took every precaution that it should not result in oppression of the poor. He worked incessantly to prevent private feuds among his nobles, because they interfered with the tilling of the soil.

His great love for the poor shines out in this passage from the *Instructions* to his son, the future Philip the Bold : "If it become needful for you to make war, be very careful that the poor people who had no part in the injustice that led to it should be preserved from all hurt, either by fire or otherwise, for it is better that you should constrain the evildoer by seizing his goods, his towns and castles, than that you should ravage the goods of the poor."

Saint Louis not only befriended the poor, but he tried to do justice to all classes without respect of persons. He was lavish in his almsgiving, and established numerous charitable foundations and hospitals ; he also defended the acquired rights of the new bourgeoisie of the communes and cities. There was sound wisdom in this policy, for it assured him of friends who would stand by him when he had to punish the injustices of his peers and barons.

So far as lay in his power, he would permit no injustice to be done, even by members of his own family. His brother, the powerful Charles of Anjou, once caused a knight to be thrown into prison because he had appealed to the king against what he considered an unjust sentence in one of Charles' courts. The king summoned his brother by royal letters, and when Charles appeared the king blamed him much for having seized the knight who had appealed. He said that there could be only one king in France, and that he must not think that because he was the king's brother, any violation of justice could be sanctioned.

On one occasion, an unfaithful wife had procured the death of her husband and pleaded deep repentance. As she belonged to one of the noble families of Pontoise, Queen Marguerite, the Countess of Pontoise and other great ladies, besought the king to remit the sentence of death. The king refused. Thereupon some of the preaching friars interceded for the guilty woman, and urged that at least the execution should not take place at Pontoise. The king consulted a wise nobleman, Simon of Nesle, and he replied that justice ought to be done publicly in the place where the crime had been committed. Accordingly the king ordered the woman to be burned publicly at Pontoise, and in spite of all appeals his orders were carried out.

In accordance with the commonly accepted principles of his time, he considered heresy to be subversive of the faith and morality of his people, and that it tended to undermine the civil order. It is especially the Albigensian heresy with which he had to deal. He counselled his son, "Do what you can to expel heretics from the land, as well as other evil people, so that it may be thoroughly purged ; do whatever you are able in this matter by the good counsel of wise and discreet men." Modern liberals and radicals, who would be the first to denounce such a policy, are strangely silent about the suppression of Christian teachers in Soviet Russia, Mexico and elsewhere. Apparently it makes a difference which kind of teachings are being suppressed.

The king's foreign policy was animated entirely by the desire to establish peace and justice. In his *Instructions* to Philip he wrote : "Dear son, I enjoin you to refrain as far as possible from war with any other Christian power. And if you are wronged by anyone, try in many ways to find some means of asserting your rights without being obliged to go to war."

His vigorous campaign against the English in

Poitou convinced the English king, Henry III, that Louis could defend his country's rights. However, in the Treaty of Paris (1258), which terminated the hostilities with the English, Louis made concessions to the English which his council opposed as giving them more than they deserved. His defence was, "As for the land which I give up, I do not give it to the English king and his heirs because I am bound to do so, but that there may be love between my children and his, who are cousins. And it seems to me that I do well to make this gift, since he was not before this my vassal, and must now do homage to me."

He also concluded a treaty of peace with Spain in 1258, and his intervention effected a reconciliation between the Emperor Frederick II and the Holy See. His love of peace was manifested not only in words, but in deeds.

There were not lacking critics who accused Louis of going too far in the direction of piety and asceticism, and intimated that his religious zeal unfitted him to be ruler of the kingdom. A woman named Salette was pleading one day in the king's court against a knight, John of Fouilleuse.

As the king came out of his chamber, this woman shouted up at him from the foot of the stairs: "Fie, fie! You ought not to be king of France. It would be much better to have another king, for you are ever busied with minor friars, preaching friars, priests and clerks : it is a great pity that you are king of France, and it is a great marvel that you have not been put out of the kingdom."

The king's sergeants were for beating the woman and chasing her out of the court, but the king forbade them, and smiling, replied to the woman's taunt : "Certainly you speak the truth, I am unworthy to be king, and if it pleased our Lord, it would have been better that another should have been king who knew better how to govern the kingdom." Thereupon he ordered one of his chamberlains to give the woman forty sous.

He was content to dismiss this woman's criticism with a smile, but he undoubtedly believed that he had a right to the consolations of religion as a compensation for the heavy burdens of his office. This is evident from his reply to a similar criticism that was commonly levelled at him by worldly nobles.

Geoffry of Beaulieu writes : "As he had heard that some of the nobles murmured against him because he attended so many masses and sermons, he replied that if he were to employ twice as much time in dice-throwing, or in ranging through the forest to hunt animals and birds, no one would make objection."

Charlemagne once said, "Of a king I expect wisdom ; of a scholar, learning ; and of a priest, piety." This gentle and playfully humorous king of France possessed all three — and wisdom supremely. Above all he had a childlike heart and retained it to the end. It is only his sanctity that can explain the superhuman results of his reign. He consolidated his kingdom and raised it to a place of pre-eminence in Europe. He made France command respect in her foreign relations. In spite of his reverses in Egypt and the Holy Land, he extended French influence in the East.

A Tartar Khan once put the question to a missionary, "Who is the greatest Western prince ?"

Without hesitation the missionary replied, "The Emperor."

"You are wrong," said the barbarian chief, "it is the king of France."

SAINT FRANCES OF ROME
[1384-1440]

I

IT would be rash to deny that Saint Frances of Rome became a saint while her husband was yet in the flesh. She died but four years after he did; and almost all her good works and mystical experiences, which made her a model to the Roman matrons of her time and inspired so many of them to live stricter and more disciplined lives, belonged to the years of her married life. She was indeed a model for women of every age and nation.

It may be true that because of the modern changes in the position of women it is easier for married women to become saints today than it was in the Middle Ages. This is alleged in an article in a recent number of *Blackfriars :*

One point is very striking : in modern times we get saintly women among the housewives — Elizabeth Leseur and Marie Christine. In the Middle Ages, the only two married saints of any note were both of royal blood, St. Margaret of Scotland and St. Elizabeth of Hungary, who (like Angela of Foligno) really only became a saint after her husband's death. Probably the explanation of this strange social phenomenon is that any trace of the slave mentality hindered the free workings of the Holy Ghost, and it was left to a more enlightened age to produce women whose husbands helped them to become saintly.[1]

This may be true as a general principle of the women of the Middle Ages ; but Saint Margaret of Scotland outlived her husband only four days, while Saint Elizabeth, as we have seen, was a saint from childhood. Saint Frances of Rome lived in the transition period between the Middle Ages and the Renaissance.

II

FRANCESCA DE BUSSI was a child precocious in her spiritual development. Owing to her mother's edifying example, she became scrupulously pious and devout at the age of six. She then began making regular confessions to an Olivetan Father of the church of Santa Maria Nuova. This White Benedictine monk, Dom Antonio, continued as her director for thirty years. The church in which she began her spiritual life is now named S. Francesca,

[1] *Woman in the Middle Ages*, by Margaret Trouncer, in "Blackfriars," Nov. 1932.

SAINT FRANCES OF ROME

and what is left of her body lies under the High Altar, exposed to public view.

From her earliest years she ate only bread and vegetables and drank only water. She manifested signs of being called to the religious life. She seemed to feel an overpowering impulse to dedicate herself to a life of virginity. When she reached the age of ten, however, her father informed her that she must put out of her head all ideas of religious vocation, as he had promised her in marriage to Lorenzo Ponziani, the son of a noble and pious Roman family.

This decision was a shattering blow to the child. She ran to her confessor and between sobs told him her sad news: in those days a mere whim of the father could settle the future destiny of a daughter and it would never have occurred to a girl of Francesca's age to question the wisdom of her father's decision. Nor did it occur to Dom Antonio to plead with the father to change his mind. He simply told Francesca that she must accept this decision of her father as the will of God.

"Is not love always a sacrifice?" he asked. "Look well into the cause of your troubles. What is your ground of complaint, my daughter? Is it the fulfilment of God's will or is it the failure of your

[131]

hopes ? Take courage, child ; think only of pleasing God and if He refuses you the honor of being His spouse, be His faithful servant in whatever state he may place you."

The highest wisdom lay hidden in those words. Married life is indeed a sacrifice for one who aspires to solitude, contemplation and frequent acts of piety ; just as the religious life is a sacrifice for those whose natural disposition inclines them to marriage. In either situation, a Christian can live a life of renunciation and obedience to the will of God.

Frances was married in her twelfth year. Lorenzo Ponziani was of a distinguished family, a Guelph, passionately devoted to the cause of the Papacy, which so many of his contemporaries had betrayed. His young bride was to find in him the qualities of uprightness and generosity. Already she could appreciate his goodness, delicacy, gentle bearing and manly sentiments. Lorenzo on the other hand was fortunate to have secured as a helpmate one so abundantly gifted with beauty, nobility, fortune and virtue. His ardent love for her, sanctified by the Sacrament of marriage, burnt as a flame which was never extinguished until his death.

Lorenzo's older brother, Paluzzo, had married Vannozza of the noble Santa Croce family. Her woman's instinct told her that Francesca was not altogether happy over her approaching marriage. A few days before the wedding day she took Frances aside and attempted to comfort her.

Frances confided to her that she had long entertained a desire for the religious life and it had been frustrated by her father's action. Vannozza took her hand and said : "I hope I may be able to comfort you, for I want you to know that I also cherish the keen desire for retirement and prayer ; if it does not displease you to accept me as your companion, from henceforth I propose to help you."

This was the beginning of a friendship which continued without mishap for thirty-eight years. They often prayed together and were familiar figures in the poorer quarters of Rome as they went forth together to minister to the poor and sick. They aimed at a sort of religious life under a common rule. When they went about on their errands of mercy, they dressed plainly, and secretly they practised bodily austerities. Later on they avoided public banquets and brilliant social functions. Their mother-in-law feared that they might injure their health and that their over-zealous conduct might bring discredit upon the family name. But when she appealed to her sons to curb the enthusiasm of their wives, they refused to interfere in any way with the religious practices and charitable work of these young women.

Their life of good works was for a time interrupted by a mysterious illness which kept Frances in bed for nearly a year. She was unable to walk and lost the power of speech. She also suffered intense pain. The cause of this illness was probably mental, arising from her profound repugnance to marriage and her grievous disappointment at not being able to enter the religious life.

The Ponziani family thought that the illness was due to some diabolical influence and suggested that magical remedies be resorted to, but the patient stubbornly resisted. Without consulting her, however, they admitted a witch to her room. Frances at once recognized the depraved character of her visitor and the power of speech suddenly returned to her. Sitting up in bed she exclaimed:

"Begone, thou servant of Satan. Do not ever dare to enter these walls again!"

She fell into a stupor and remained unconscious far into the night. Towards morning, when her attendants, weary with watching, had fallen asleep, a bright light shone about her bed and Saint Alexius appeared to Frances in a vision. He asked her if she was prepared to die or if she wished to recover.

She answered that she wished only to do what God willed. The Saint informed her that it was God's will that she be restored to health and spend her life for His greater glory. Thereupon the vision vanished.

Frances arose and dressed herself without assistance, and tiptoing into Vanozza's room, shook her and exclaimed that she was cured. They escaped from the house together before anyone was up, and hastened to the nearby church of Saint Alexius, whose feast day it was. Frances wished first of all to render thanks for her recovery in the presence of the relics of the young Roman patrician of the fifth century who, according to the popular legend, had fled from his bride on the night of his marriage and lived for seventeen years as a hermit in the East. He had always been a favorite saint with Frances. On the eve of his feast, therefore, it was not strange that he should have appeared to her in a vision, and restored her miraculously to health.

Frances was henceforth more reconciled to married life, and exerted herself to perform her duties as the wife of a Roman nobleman and head of a large household. By divine intervention she had learned that marriage need not diminish one's interior grace and that Almighty God is not to be categorically limited in the distribution of His favors to any class or station in life. Furthermore she prayed that she might have children in order that she might give saints to Heaven.

In 1400, two years after her marriage, her first child was born. He was baptized Giovanni Battista in the church of Saint Cecilia, which was near the Ponziani palace. Frances modified her manner of life in order that she might devote herself to the nursing of her son. Her father rejoiced as he held his long wished-for grandson in his arms, and died but a few days later. Her mother-in-law also died and her widowed husband and two sons unanimously chose Frances to be the head of the household, although Vannozza should have been given the precedence, as her husband was the older. The Ponziani palace, being the headquarters of the Guelph party, was one of the best known houses in Rome. Frances presided graciously over her long table, at which the guests often numbered more than twenty. They little suspected that under her resplendent gowns she wore a hair-shirt.

In 1403 she gave birth to another son, Giovanni Evangelista. He was her favorite child, but unfortunately became a victim to the pestilence and died at the early age of ten. In 1406 the last child, Agnese, was born. Her mother had a vision which seemed to indicate that this child was destined for the religious life. She must have misinterpreted this vision, for Agnese died in her sixteenth year.

In the forty years that she lived with her husband, so it is said, there was never a dispute or quarrel between them. She put her family obligations first in her life. She gave orders to her servants to summon her whenever her husband had need of her, even if she was at Mass at Santa Maria Nuova or at prayer in her oratory. She had no hesitation in laying aside any spiritual occupation when household duties required it. It was one of her notable sayings that, "it is most laudable in a married woman to be devout, but she must never forget that she is a housewife ; and sometimes she must leave God at the altar to find Him in her housekeeping."

Life was not easy in the Ponziani palace and it required superhuman strength to preserve peace and love in a home that was set in the midst of so many miseries and calamities. Leagues and counter-plots, assassinations, poisonings, recourse to magic, exile, violent death — such were common events in the Rome of the fifteenth century. It was the period of the exile of the Popes at Avignon, and in Rome there was constant plotting of antipopes and false popes. Ladislas of Naples, the ally of one antipope, often sent troops to invade the city ; famine and epidemics added their ravages to the sufferings of

the inhabitants. At such times Frances and Vannozza distributed food to hundreds of starving
families.

In 1408 the troops of Ladislas of Naples entered
Rome, and Count Troja — a rough soldier of fortune — was appointed Governor. In the street fighting which ensued, Lorenzo Ponziani was stabbed and
his apparently lifeless body was carried home to his
wife. He was brought back to life by her loving
care and devotion.

Later when Troja was compelled to withdraw his
army from Rome, he sought to avenge himself on
some of the chief papal families. He took Lorenzo
prisoner and demanded as the price of his liberty that
his son Battista, then a little boy of eight, be handed
over to him as an hostage. When Frances heard
the news she was horrified and determined to take
her son out of the city to a place of safety. As she
and the boy were escaping, they met her confessor,
Dom Antonio, and he bade her take the boy to the
capital and deliver him up as an hostage. She re-
luctantly obeyed and retired to the church of
Ara Coeli, where she threw herself down before the
altar of Our Lady and pleaded for her son. The
story runs that they put the boy on the horse of one
of Troja's knights before the rider, but the horse
refused to move. Other horses were tried and they

likewise baulked. Finally Troja gave orders to restore the boy to his family.

In 1410, Rome was again captured and pillaged by the soldiers of Ladislas. The Cardinals were assembled at Bologna for the election of a new Pope. Lorenzo, being one of the heads of the papal party, was in danger from the invading army. He escaped from Rome, but his wife and children had to remain behind. Battista was taken prisoner, but later he too escaped and joined his father. The Ponziani palace was plundered by the soldiers of Ladislas, and the family possessions in the Campagna were burned and their farms ruined and the flocks slaughtered. Many of their tenants were murdered. When Vannozza's husband was taken prisoner, she lived with Frances and Evangelista and Agnese in a corner of the ruined palace — the two women devoting themselves to the children and offering such aid as they could to their less fortunate neighbors.

Three years later Rome was further devastated by famine and pestilence. Evangelista, who was then only ten and had already developed into a saint, was stricken by the disease and died. Frances thereupon turned part of their house into a hospital and God bestowed upon her the gift of healing.

I⊤ will always be a problem for married women who live in the midst of worldly society and yet faithfully discharge their obligations to their families and neighbors, how to find strength and time for the exercises of religion, to say nothing of becoming well informed on the doctrines and history of the Church.

Saint Frances of Rome solved the problem, partly because she was an exceptionally strong-minded young woman. It is difficult to understand how even she, in so agitated a life, could have found opportunity for study and meditation. Yet during the years of her married life, while she educated her children, directed her many servants and often worked with them, cared for the plague-stricken, distributed alms and radiated good cheer generally, she at the same time studied profoundly the dogmas and history of the Church. The recitation of the Divine Office was her daily nourishment and her mind became saturated with texts from the liturgy. The Epistles of St. Paul, the homilies of Saint Gregory the Great, the prophecies of Isaias were as familiar to her as the Gospels. She meditated daily on the Psalms in the manner prescribed by Saint

Benedict, who advocated a meditative and prayerful reading of the sentences of Holy Scripture.[1]

The pious women and young girls who frequented the church of Santa Maria Nuova and saw the Donna Ponziani kneeling motionless in prayer, were prompted to ask her this question :

"How without quitting the world and our obligations may we approach nearer to the Lord and serve Him more perfectly ?"

As it had been through the Olivetan Benedictine Fathers that Frances had first learned the secret of interior peace, she conceived the idea of affiliating with this Order, as Oblates, a group of women living in the world who desired to keep a special rule of prayer and spend their leisure hours in visiting the poor and sick. This group of secular Oblates soon found it necessary to bind some of their members together as regular Oblates. Frances took the initiative in this new development. She did not hesitate to found a religious community into which she herself could not enter !

On the feast of the Annunciation 1433 the members of this new Order took up their residence in the Tor di Specchi (Tower of Mirrors). They

---

[1] *Ste. Françoise Romaine*, by Marguerie Aron, in "La Vie Spirituelle," May 1, 1932, p. 157.

first called themselves the Benedictine Oblates of Mary, but later came to be known as the Oblates of the Tor di Specchi. All Rome goes to see them on the feast day of Saint Frances, March 9, in the ancient group of buildings opposite the church of the Ara Coeli — though one looks in vain for a tower or mirrors. The house originally belonged to the Specchi family, who had on their crest three silver mirrors framed in gold. The Oblates bought it in 1443 along with the cloister and the contiguous buildings for one hundred and fifty florins.

The Oblates wear a dark habit, simple and modest, such as those worn by Roman women who were widows or dedicated their lives to good works. Their heads were covered with black mantles which they held with their hands under the chin, framing the features of a face worn with years and suffering or aglow with the splendor of youth — in either case refined by a deep spirituality. For five centuries these women have edified Roman society by their fruitful and exemplary lives. A list of their members would include most of the names that have been the glory of the Roman aristocracy from the fifteenth century to the present day, such as the Panfili, Orsini, Mignanelli, Lancelloti, Amadei, Celsi, Fani, Ruspoli and many others.

The Abbot of the Olivetan Fathers declared that they would share all the privileges accorded to the monks of the Order, participate in their pious and meritorious works, be prayed for by the monks after their death and have the right of burial in the church of Santa Maria Nuova. The discreet and generous spirit of the Benedictine rule, combining action with contemplation, inspired these holy women who in emulation of the example of Saint Frances have perpetuated her beneficent activities both within and without the House of the Tor di Specchi.

In this house Frances took up her abode after the death of her husband in 1436. She lived with and governed her spiritual daughters, directing them in the ways of fruitful Benedictine sanctity until she was called to receive her reward in Heaven. Up to the time she entered that house, she was faithful to her duties at home, as Lorenzo had besought her to live under his roof until his death, although he released her from her marital obligations. Whatever time she could spare from her household tasks she spent with her beloved Oblates sharing with them the most menial tasks.

Lorenzo was completely broken in health and though his property had been restored to him after he returned from banishment, the prizes of this world had lost their savor. His wife ministered to him with the utmost devotion and left nothing undone to prepare him for a holy death.

Among her other trials, Frances experienced to the full the criticisms and opposition that may come from a daughter-in-law with a violent and over-bearing temper. Battista had married a beautiful girl by the name of Mobilia. She treated her mother-in-law with the utmost contempt, complained of her actions both to her husband and his father, and in public ridiculed her pious practices and her reputation for sanctity. This antagonism between daughter-in-law and mother-in-law did not however follow the conventional lines. In the midst of a bitter tirade of criticism against Frances, Mobilia was one day stricken with a severe illness. Frances nursed her and brought her back to life. Mobilia's contempt turned into love and henceforth she strove to imitate the holy life of the saint. When Frances went to live with the Oblates, Battista and his wife pleaded earnestly with her not to leave them.

v

FRANCES was a woman of unusual mystical gifts. She was favored with visions which took the form of dramas of heavenly characters, whose purpose was to reveal to her a necessary truth or inspire her to perform an action for the good of the Church. She was frequently seen in a state of ecstasy after receiving Holy Communion in the church of Santa Maria Nuova, and it is said that only her confessor could arouse her from this state of ecstatic prayer. She also had the power to read the secrets of consciences and to detect diabolical plots.

One of the characteristic features of her mystical life was an ability to perceive the presence of angels. Such faculty is difficult for us to understand, not only because we rarely hear of modern saints, who enjoyed this privilege, but also because angels are by the dogmatic teaching of the Church to be understood as purely spiritual beings. When they manifested themselves to men of old, as in the many instances recorded in Holy Scripture, they assumed temporarily a bodily form.

A year after the death of her favorite son, Evangelista, while Frances was praying in her private oratory, a bright light suddenly shone before her and she saw the departed child accompanied by an archangel. The boy told her of his happiness in Heaven and foretold the approaching death of his sister Agnese, which actually happened as he had foretold. He consoled his mother, however, by informing her that the archangel who accompanied him was henceforth to be her guide. For twenty-three years this archangel was nearly always visible to Frances, though invisible to those about her. He assumed the form of a beautiful child of eight or thereabouts and indicated his wishes by touching her shoulder or, when she needed restraining, striking her on the cheek. When she committed a fault the angel vanished, but returned when she made her confession. In the last epoch of her life this angel was succeeded by another of still higher dignity.

All this sounds to many of us like an old wives' fable. There is no difficulty in believing that each one of us has a guardian angel; and there is no reason why we should not speak to our guardian angels more often than we do. The modern student is tempted to believe that Frances was in the habit of talking familiarly with her guardian angel and that thus there grew up the tradition that the angel was visible to her. One can imagine the tradition gradually becoming more embellished until finally we have the charming description of the child-like figure of great sweetness and beauty, with eyes turned towards heaven and hands folded on his breast, who wore a long shining robe and over it a tunic "which was sometimes white like the lilies, sometimes red-rose, and sometimes blue like the sky."

No doubt it would add much to the picturesqueness and poetry of life if we could all have even occasional glimpses of our guardian angels; and most of us would welcome a slap on the cheek now and then to warn us that we were on the wrong track. However, there is nothing intrinsically impossible in the fact that such a saint as Frances of Rome was favored with a heavenly attendant who was always visible to her. If Tobias had the assistance of an angel in discovering useful medicines in the entrails of a fish, why should not Frances have such assistance in — shall we say ? — more important works ? Perhaps it is well that angels do not appear to us as we go about our tasks. Saint Bridget said : "If we saw an angel clearly, we should die of pleasure ; if it were a demon, we should die of fright and horror."

Mystics have received revelations, sometimes by means of locutions — auricular, imaginative or intellectual — at other times by means of visions which may be exterior, imaginative or intellectual. The revelations which Saint Frances enjoyed usually came by way of mystical vision. She beheld saints and angels, as we have already seen. When she recovered from the plague after her family had given up hope, she had a vision of hell so terrible that she could never speak of it without tears. She also saw clearly into the meaning of many contemporary historical events and what would be their ultimate results.

M. Ernest Hello in his *Physionomie des Saints*[1] remarks that the life of Saint Frances may be summed up in one word, namely, *vision*. He says: "For her to live was to see. Her life in this world was like a light and transparent veil, covering the life which she already lived in the other world. Her earthly life seems almost like an apparition."

The times in which she lived were replete with calamities and distresses: civil war, pestilence, famine, brigandage and the wanton destruction of property, filled the hearts of the Roman people with anxiety and terror. The Eternal City in those days presented an utter contrast to the Rome of the present day with its ordered government and amicable relations between Church and State.

Yet Frances went about the streets of that stricken city, tranquil and unharmed. Not only was she universally respected for her works of mercy, her miracles and her extraordinary virtue; but as her heart was in heaven, she had nothing to fear on earth. She looked not on the things which were seen, but on the things which were not seen. Her gaze was fixed on the unchanging eternal realities.

The year 1434 was marked by unusual misfor-

[1] P. 89.

tunes. The Pope, Eugenius IV, was in exile. As he had taken the side of the Florentines in their war with Philip, Duke of Milan, Philip in revenge had stirred up against the Pope many of the bishops, assembled in the Council of Basle. They even dared to summon the Pope to appear before the Council as an accused criminal.

On the night of the 14th of October, Frances was in an ecstasy in her oratory. The Mother of God appeared to her and gave her instructions to be transmitted to the Pope at Bologna. The next day Frances called on her confessor Dom Giovanni, and besought him to go at once to Bologna to carry out the orders of Our Lady. He demurred, saying that his journey would be useless; that he would only compromise Frances and himself; and that the Pope would look upon him as a fool and a dupe.

However, as Frances insisted, he went and was received cordially by the Pope, who approved of all the requests that Frances had sent, and gave orders that they be carried out.

When Dom Giovanni returned and began to describe to her the results of his mission, she interrupted him, saying:

"It is I, if you please, who will recount to you the events of your journey. I was with you in spirit; and I know all that has happened."

She narrated the facts exactly as they had taken place, among them the recovery of a member of the party from an illness, due to the prayers of Frances.

Already two women, Saint Bridget of Sweden and Saint Catherine of Siena, had been used by the Holy Spirit as messengers to the Popes to urge them to return from Avignon to the Chair of Saint Peter, and among temporal disasters and historical disorders, to help clarify their sense of divine mission. Saint Frances, too, had a part to play in this drama. She saw that the bishops assembled at Basle, as well as many priests and religious, because blinded by political passions were falling into error. It was in the darkness of this terrible time when so many enemies were rising up against the Church that Saint Joan of Arc was burned at the stake in Rouen.

Frances spent long vigils in prayer for the Church. Her prophets and saints revealed to her the dangers of the present and future. She was finally spurred to action, first under the inspiration of Saint Thomas the Apostle, and then under that of Saint Gregory the Great ; and she dictated to her confessor some letters to the Pope. She urged the Holy Father not to let himself be deceived or trust to appearances or insist on little things ; that he seek not his own advantage, but give attention rather to the flock which had been committed to him and for which he would have to render an account.

In the midst of the general confusion she built up through her Oblates a rampart of prayer about the Pope and Rome. She said to her spiritual daughters :

It is for you to supply what is lacking in others. It is your vocation to pray and do penance for yourselves and for them. You are the victims destined to appease the Divine anger ; and your tears must extinguish this conflagration. . . Through you, Rome will recover peace and liberty. The Madonna will call you indeed her Oblates, when she sees you thus offering your souls and bodies as an oblation to the Most High.[1]

On the 13th of August 1439, Frances perceived a change in the visage and bearing of her Guardian Angel. His face glowed with joy as he said :

"I am going to weave a veil of a hundred strands, then another of sixty, then another of thirty."

One hundred and ninety days after the vision, the Angel had completed his task. The face of Frances was seen to shine with an unearthly light. The end of her strenuous and agitated life was at hand. Her last words were :

"The Angel has finished his task : he beckons me to follow him."

[1] *Ste. Françoise Romaine*, in "La Vie Spirituelle," May 1, 1922, p. 160.

BLESSED NICHOLAS OF FLÜE
[1417-1487]

THE man who in middle life breaks away from the assumed responsibilities of his earlier years, and sets out on an entirely new adventure has been a favorite theme of contemporary novelists and dramatists. When a man of the world, without deeply rooted religious convictions, does this sort of thing, we are not surprised ; but we hardly expect it of a saint. He, of all men, we like to think, would patiently fulfil the duties of the state in life to which God had called him — unless and until God called him to another.

Nicholas of Flüe, who came as near as any one to being the patron saint of Switzerland, had as soldier, peasant, patriot and judge, endeared himself to his fellow-countrymen. He had married and become the father of ten children. Fourteen months after the birth of his last child, he forsook his wife and children and spent the last twenty years of his life as a hermit, in almost perpetual prayer. Yet he was beatified by the Church, and doubtless would have been canonized had not the documents relating

to his process of canonization been destroyed by a
fire in the Vatican.

I

As a young man, Nicholas fought in several wars in
defence of the liberties of the Swiss Confederates,
especially against the Hapsburgs. For centuries his
family had been among the most honored of the
landowners and peasants of the Unterwald. They
lived near Sachseln, on the lake of Sarnen, not far
from Lucerne. After the siege of Zurich, Nicholas
received a commission in the army, and used his
authority and personal influence for the scrupulous
observance of the Convention of Sempach, which
pledged the armies of the Confederates to respect
churches, chapels and monasteries; and to spare
women, children, and the clergy. A contemporary
says of him : "He was a friend of peace, a defender
of widows and orphans ; he was merciful and ex-
horted the others to show mercy." He fought with
a sword in one hand, and a rosary in the other !

Although from his earliest years he loved solitude
and prayer, he did not feel that they would be in-
consistent with his duties as head of a Christian family ; therefore he was quite willing at the suggestion
of his parents to marry and carry on the family tra-

dition.　As he was quite unlettered, it never occurred
to him that he might have a call to the priesthood
or the religious life.

He chose for his wife the pious and comely
daughter of one of the chief families of Sachseln,
Dorothea Wysling.　He was twenty-one when they
married, and in thirty years his wife bore him ten
children :　John, Rudolph, Walter, Henry, Nicholas, Dorothea, Marguerite, Katherine, Veronica,
and another daughter who died in infancy, and whose
name has been lost.　John, the eldest, was elected
Landmann of the Unterwald.　Nicholas, the youngest, after studying at the Universities of Basle and
Paris, became a priest and was for many years parish
priest of Sachseln.　The oldest daughter, Dorothea,
was highly esteemed by her contemporaries for her
piety, and was called "the consolation of the
Church."

The house built by Nicholas, on his extensive
domain, still stands.　It is of wood, and one roof
covers both the dwelling-house and the stable, the
one facing west and the other east.　The door opens
upon a sort of hall, at one end of which is the fireplace designed for the preparation of food.　From
the chimney over the fireplace the smoke found its
way as it could to an opening in the roof.　From
this hall one passes to the vast living-room, on a

little higher level. A small window gave the only light. Here the family assembled for meals, and the parents slept. Besides the primitive four-poster bed, its furniture consisted of a great earthen stove, a long table, with massive benches on either side fastened to the floor, a buffet and some wooden stools. The only ornament on the wall was a huge crucifix. A rude staircase led to the floor above, where the children and servants slept. Such was the luxury of a prosperous Swiss peasant in the fifteenth century.

Nicholas was the first to rise, and when the dawn broke was calling out his flocks and leading them to pasture on the hills. In summer he worked in the fields. The chief part of the day's arduous tasks were over when he sat down with his family to dinner at nine in the morning. The servants ate at the same table with the master's family. When the day's work was done, they came together again for the final repast, called *Vesperbrod*. The evening, long or short according to the season, ended with family prayers.

We can imagine this sturdy laborer, kneeling on the hard floor with his household at the close of the day, commending to the Lord the souls that had been given into his care. Like the patriarchs of old, he looked across the generations and the centuries, and saw the stream of divine grace bringing strength to countless men and women yet unborn. Races are fashioned from the souls of their ancestors, even more than from their blood.

While working in the fields he was often rapt in an ecstasy of prayer. Since his marriage, he continued to practice the frequent fasts he had begun in his youth ; and at such times he sought solitude far away from frequented places, where he could enter into intimate communion with God.

In 1460, when the Austrian Archduke Sigismund attempted to invade the Swiss Cantons, Nicholas was in command of a company of a hundred men in the army that defended the country. The Swiss repulsed the Austrians, and pursued them into Thurgovia, which was subdued in a few weeks. The little village of Diesenhofer resisted long and valiantly. When finally the Swiss Confederates had succeeded in capturing it, many Austrian soldiers sought refuge in the church of the Dominican Convent of Saint Catherine. The Swiss command decided to disregard the Convention of Sempach, and gave orders to set fire to the church.

When Nicholas heard of this dastardly decision, he ran to the convent and saw at once the grave danger to which the nuns were exposed. He fell on his knees before the great crucifix in the cloister, and pleaded for divine guidance. Then he hastened to the Council of War and passionately besought the leaders to revoke their order. He laid stress on the moral gravity of their act, the frightful results that would ensue, and prophesied with evident inspiration the countless examples of heroic virtue which during the coming centuries this convent would inspire. The sacrilegious order was cancelled, and Nicholas commissioned to make sure of the safety of the convent. The fire had already made some headway, but he was able to check it, and thereby saved the convent, the church and the soldiers who had fled there for sanctuary. This convent stood until 1869, and the holy Nicholas of Flüe was always honored as its savior. The crucifix before which he prayed was preserved as a precious relic. His prophecy was verified by the heroic resistance with which these Dominican nuns met the propaganda and persecution of the Reformation era.

When peace was declared, a gold medal was given Nicholas as a token of the national gratitude for his services. It bore the image of a porcupine, and the inscription: "One who has the strength of an army." His distinguished services in the war commended him more than ever to his fellow-citizens for the office of Landmann or chief magistrate. He had refused it when it had been offered him on a previous occasion. Now once again he insisted that "he could consider only as enemies of his repose and of his conscience those who made him such proposals." Already, no doubt, he had intimations that God had other designs for his future. He said, "One is more safe on the low ground than on the heights; to be judge of the business and affairs of the world easily disturbs the heart of man."

He willingly served, however, in the office of judge for the canton when his turn came. A contemporary writer speaks thus of the judicial qualities of his mind : "A noble simplicity ruled his speech. He displayed such balance of judgment in the cases brought before him that his decision immediately convinced every one as being right. His spirit of justice and impartiality, as well as his reputation for piety and mercy, had gained for him widespread confidence, and he was often chosen arbiter in serious controversies."

Some of the more influential citizens of the Unterwald once refused to accept his decision, and persuaded the other judges of the court to reverse his judgment. A humble peasant had borrowed a large sum of money from a rich neighbor, pledging as security a garden of much greater value than the loan. When the debtor was ready to repay the loan and take back the title to his property, the rich creditor refused to surrender his right to the garden, claiming that it had been sold to him. The case came before the tribunal where Nicholas presided along with several other judges. He ruled that each should take back what belonged to him — the one his garden, the other his money. The creditor would not agree to this, and as he belonged to a powerful family he was able to exert pressure on the other judges so that they gave judgment in his favor. After this Nicholas retired from office, saying that he would have nothing more to do with the justice of men. Later he testified that he could see and feel flames of fire, of a disgusting odor, issuing from the mouths of the judges as they pronounced their unjust sentence; and he knew that they already had a foretaste of hell within themselves.

From that day there began to develop in the community a coterie hostile to Nicholas of Flüe. His enemies did what they could to discredit his exceptional virtue, and caricatured him as a fanatical, fantastic individual who was striving to acquire a reputation for sanctity and win the confidence of his fellow-citizens. In spite of these calumnies, though he had ceased to be an official judge, he was often selected as arbiter by the mass of his neighbors to settle difficult quarrels. Even from the adjoining cantons men came to seek his opinions and counsel. It was plain to all men of good will that God had endowed him with supreme wisdom, and they knew that he would never violate his conscience or regard the persons of men.

If Nicholas had been convinced that it was God's will that he continue to fulfil the duties incumbent on him as husband and father, citizen and judge, no opposition or criticism could have driven him into retirement. As the years went on, it was becoming increasingly clear to him that his work in the world was done, and that God was calling him to perform a task on an entirely different plane. As he approached his fiftieth year, he felt daily an irresistible attraction toward a state of life that more closely approximated the life of heaven. He longed for solitude and the opportunity for continuous prayer. He had trodden the rough paths of the purgative way, and was now well along in the illuminative stage of the mystical life. God favored him with visions which left him in no doubt as to what he would have him do.

II

In 1467, Nicholas prayed God to grant him the grace to live in complete union with him. In response he heard the command to abandon himself utterly to the divine will. He immediately made known the terms of this divine vocation to his wife. Though completely overcome by the news, she would not permit herself to put obstacles in the way of his obeying God's call, and forthwith gave her consent. As a good Catholic, Nicholas knew that he had no right to withdraw from his obligations to his wife and children without her free authorization. She wept as she made the supreme sacrifice.

Together Nicholas and his saintly wife drew up an agreement concerning the education of their children, the administration of their property and the future direction of the affairs of the household. Then Nicholas called in his children and servants and made known to them his decision. In their presence he solemnly invested his wife with his parental authority and constituted her the head of the family.

Brother Klaus, as he was known from that day, set forth as a pilgrim, clad in a rough habit and carrying only a staff, to seek a hermitage where he might spend the remainder of his days. He walked many miles in the direction of Basle, and at sunset came upon an unknown peasant who consented to give him lodging for the night. As he explained to the man his quest for a place of solitude, the peasant said, "The mountains of your own country must contain many deserted spots, where you would be free to pray, and yet remain near those in the midst of whom God caused you to be born."

After the evening meal and a few hours of repose, Brother Klaus went out to pray under the stars, and weigh before God the counsel he had received from the peasant. He determined to accept it as coming from a heavenly source.

Suddenly he felt in his heart and then throughout his whole body an agonizing pain, as if some vital organ had been taken from him. He has left his own description of this experience : "A light from heaven seemed to surround me, and I felt in my intestines a violent pain, as if someone had first probed them with a sharp knife and then cut them out. From that instant, I have never felt the need of human food or drink, and have never used them."

Henceforth he was established in a new state of life, and set wholly free from all that excites the desires and passions of men.

Taking up his staff, he returned to his own neighborhood. He finally selected Ranft, on the banks of a mountain gorge, overlooking Sachseln and the Lake of Sarnen, and not far from his own home ; and there he dwelt for the remaining twenty years of his life.

The fact that he never ate or drank anything except the Blessed Sacrament soon became known to the whole countryside. Many spies were sent out to watch him and see if they could not detect him bringing food to his hermitage, perhaps in the night. But they found no evidence of his taking either food or drink. When people questioned him about it, he never said definitely that he never took any food. He preferred to say that he never took any human food. He often quoted the saying of our Lord, "Man doth not live by bread only, but by every word that proceedeth out of the mouth of God."

When Thomas, the vicar-general and coadjutor of the Bishop of Constance visited Brother Klaus to consecrate the chapel which his neighbors had built for him, they conferred together for several hours on spiritual subjects. The bishop asked him which of the virtues he considered the most excellent and the most pleasing to God. Brother Klaus replied that he considered holy obedience the highest virtue.

The bishop approved of his answer, and then took a morsel of bread and a little wine and said to Nicholas, "Here, my brother, is the nourishment and the beverage which obedience presents to you."

Brother Klaus had taken no food or drink for eighteen months and was dismayed at the command, and begged that this test might be spared him. The bishop insisting, he asked that he might cut the bread into three minute fragments. The bishop consented, and Brother Klaus put one of them into his mouth. His throat was so dry and contracted that he had great difficulty in swallowing it. Soon he was seized with a fit of choking, and it seemed as though he might choke to death.

The bishop was overwhelmed with fright and compassion and asked Brother Klaus' pardon, declaring to those present that he had acted only according to the express order of the Bishop of Constance. He became firmly convinced of Brother Klaus' abstinence, and made to his superior a faithful report of all that he had witnessed.

Brother Klaus had at first built a hut of branches of trees to shelter him from the elements. After his chapel was built, he could see the altar from a window which communicated with the adjoining hut. Through this window he received the Blessed Sacrament every morning. Until he had a chaplain, he attended Mass on Sundays and holy days in the parish church of Sachseln. In 1470 Pope Paul II granted the first indulgence to the sanctuary at Ranft, and it became a place of pilgrimage.

Occasionally the hermit left his solitude to make a pilgrimage to Engleberg or Einsiedeln. He took part in the procession of the Incarnation every year at Lucerne on March 25. In the intervals Brother Klaus led a regular life, rising at midnight and re-

maining in prayer till the following noon. Then
he walked along the ravine or in the forest which
bordered on it ; and in the years when Brother Ul-
rich lived with him, he would converse with him or
receive the numerous visitors who came each afternoon. Toward evening he again took up his work
of prayer, which was interrupted only by a few
hours of repose.

Not only was he visited by important personages,
who have left interesting accounts of their talks with
him, but he gladly received also the poor and humble
and little children. As in the days of John the Baptist, the desert again attracted the multitudes in quest
of words from heaven. Pilgrims came from all
parts of Christendom, — many inspired only by curiosity, but the majority to seek counsel, consolation,
or prophecies of the future, from one who seemed
to them a faithful interpreter of the word of God.
He welcomed with joy and tenderness his Swiss compatriots, who had come to look upon him as their
national saint, as the presence of God made visible
in their midst. To each group of pilgrims he spoke
with fatherly kindness, addressing them with such
words as he thought they most needed to hear.

For example, this man who had so long lived as
a faithful husband and father, could speak with authority to married people : "The married ought to

fulfil the duties of their state in the fear of God, and concern themselves in peace and according to the laws of justice with the care of their family. They should act faithfully from the love of God and their neighbor, and remain unshakable in their piety. Each state of life has its special duties; by their accomplishment one may find happiness in the world as well as in solitude, for not all are called to separate themselves from the society of men, like John the Forerunner, and to lead in the desert a solitary life."

This man who had so many years of experience as a father also knew how to speak to children: "Never forget the all-powerful God, but remain in his presence; and serve him with attention and devotion. Whatever you do or suffer, let your life be directed toward him; consecrate it entirely to the sovereign Lord. Let your acts and adventures be regulated by his will and commands. It is he who gives and takes away, who blesses and condemns; worship him.

"He who aspires to the grace of God must be pure, with a heart as innocent as a child's. Purity of heart is to God like a perfume sweet and agreeable.

"The fear of God and obedience to their parents win for children blessing and a long life."

Sometimes when the crowd of pilgrims was greater than usual and he found himself addressing people of all ages and conditions, he felt as if he were speaking to all his countrymen and his words were inspired.   On one such occasion, he said :

My sons and my daughters, give heed to your pastors and the guides of your souls, learn from them the Christian truth, accept their warnings and fulfil as perfectly as possible all that they command you to do and believe.   Be like obedient lambs to your lawful spiritual shepheards. Thus you will always know the divine will.   Listen to them as you would listen to Christ, the supreme Pastor who is in the midst of you through his Church and will continue to be until the end of the world.

Fear and love God above all things and try to keep always a pure conscience, for nothing in all the world is better or more precious ; it is the most sumptuous garment of men.   When the mind and the heart are good, all is good.

And when your conscience is soiled by sin, ask of God the grace of repentance, and endeavor without delay to purify yourselves by confession and penance.

To order one's life properly, one must always think of being able to end it with a peaceful conscience, for it is more frightful and terrible to fall into the hand of the eternal Judge than to undergo the most intense bodily sufferings.

Be sober and hard-working men ; avoid all vanity in dress which will exclude you from heaven ; try to keep to the simplicity of manners of our fathers.

Keep toward your compatriots and toward foreigners a sincere fraternal charity and a Christian loyalty.

If you are tried by adversity, bear it with patience and remember that it is the will of God.

O man, believe in God with all your might, for hope rests on faith, love on hope, and victory on love ; the reward will follow victory, the crown of life the reward, but the crown is the essence of things eternal.

The wife and children of Brother Klaus frequently attended Mass in his chapel, and were at times among the pilgrims who listened to his words of spiritual counsel. When need arose, they did not hesitate to seek his advice in their personal difficulties or the affairs of the household.

The crowning instance of the powerful influence wielded by Brother Klaus over the hearts of his countrymen was when the national unity was threatened by a prolonged disagreement between the rural and urban cantons at the Diet of Stanz. After the victory over the forces of the Duke of Burgundy, the city cantons under the leadership of Berne conceived the design of making the Swiss Confederacy a powerful European state which would occupy the central place dreamed of by Charles the Bold. The men of the rural cantons opposed this plan at the Diet of Stanz in 1481, and many days of furious debate ended only in a deadlock. No one was able to suggest any solution which would save the national unity.

The curé of Stanz, Henri Im Grund, who was a friend of Brother Klaus, thought to himself, "Nicholas is the only man who can — if it please God — save the country." On a cold winter night of December 21, this old priest set out through the snow and after a perilous journey reached the hermitage of Brother Klaus and acquainted him with the state of affairs.

"Return to Stanz," said Nicholas, "reassemble the delegates of the Confederation and tell them that Brother Klaus — he also — has a communication to make to them." The priest returned with quickened zeal, and reached Stanz before daybreak. He went to the hotels and persuaded the delegates not to depart until they had heard the message from Brother Klaus.

In the morning the astonished delegates reassembled, and the old hermit arrived, staff in hand, at the entrance to the city. He walked through the principal street, saluting as he passed the surprised inhabitants. He suddenly appeared in the midst of the assembly and made a speech which revealed an accurate knowledge of all the points at issue in the controversy.

He accused them of having forgotten God who had given them victory in so many wars. He urged the rural cantons to admit to the federation the cities

MARRIED SAINTS

of Fribourg and Soleure — which they had refused
to do hitherto — and the urban cantons not to ex-
tend the limits of the country further than was necessary to conserve its peace and unity. He closed his
address with this appeal :

Do not charge yourselves with too many affairs of the
outside world, and make no alliances with foreign powers.
Do not accept, dear Confederates, gifts or subsidies of
money, lest you seem to have sold your fatherland for gold,
lest envy and egotism take root amongst you and poison
your hearts. Conserve in all your relations your natural
rights ; share the spoils of victory according to the services,
and the conquered lands according to the localities. Do not
ever let yourselves be drawn into unjust wars for the hope
of pillage ; live in peace and good will with your neighbors.
If they attack you, defend the fatherland valiantly and
fight like men of courage. Practice justice in your own
borders and love one another as Christian allies. Do not
mix in foreign wars, and show yourselves invincible to
those who try to oppress you. Above all, avoid controversy.

Dear Confederates, I do not wish to leave Stanz until
you shake hands with each other like good Swiss as a sign
of reconciliation. May Almighty God bless you, and may
he protect your cities and your fields, and may he always be propitious to you as he has been to this day, and may
he be with you for all eternity.

This speech of the holy hermit worked a miracle.
The delegates forgot their divisions and gathered
round him arm in arm and cried "Long live Brother

[170]

Nicholas!" He answered, "Long live Jesus, long live His holy Name!" And then he returned as suddenly as he had come, to his hermitage. He had saved the Confederacy from disunion and destruction.

Brother Klaus entered once again into his solitude. We can see him throwing himself on his knees and pouring out his soul in the prayer which he used almost continuously: "My Lord and my God, take from me all that separates me from thee! My Lord and my God, give me everything that will bring me closer to thee! My Lord and my God, protect me from myself, and grant that I may belong entirely to thee!"

Did Nicholas commit a sin in leaving his wife and children for the life of solitude? After all marriage was his vocation. If he had remained in the world, he might have been the constant guide and companion of his growing children. He might have been elected to high office in the state, and thus have rendered inestimable service to his countrymen.

The subsequent fate of his wife and children does not indicate that they were any the worse for his becoming a hermit. He evidently had overwhelming evidence that God had called him to a different state of life. God's favors are gratuitous, and he

[171]

bestows them where he will. Who shall say that he did not accomplish more for his family by his prayers and his spiritual counsel than if he had continued to live with them? As it was, he became the savior of his country; his words could not have had such a dynamic effect if he had been merely one of the delegates at Stanz.

Through his mystical, solitary life he established continuous contact with God; he explored unknown supernatural heights, and inspired innumerable men and women to persevere in the search for spiritual realities. We do not think of blaming such men as Scott, Peary, Amundsen and Byrd for leaving their families, and setting out on perilous polar explorations in the interests of science. They have made us familiar with regions where no man can ever live. Shall we blame this man for exploring the borderland of eternity, which some day we all hope to attain?

No human adventure can be more useful than that made by brave spirits, who at the call of God have set out on the mystic way and as the fruit of their experience have given to their fellow men assurances of the reality of the supernatural world and the immensities of the divine perfections.

SAINT THOMAS MORE
[1478-1535]

I

SIR THOMAS MORE was a man of intensely domestic
tastes, loving his home and family supremely; yet
he was an intimate of the king, Henry the Eighth,
who often required his presence at court, and sent
him on important missions in England and abroad.
There can be no question where his heart was. He
cared nothing for the patronage of kings or the honors of this world. The life at court did not attract
him. He was happiest in the bosom of his family:
wife, son and daughters, sons-in-law and daughter-
in-law, and ten or more grandchildren, who all lived
in one house at Chelsea; and in the congenial group
of poets, scientists and humanists that often assembled in his home.

Henry the Eighth in his best days was a man of
rare personal magnetism, and Sir Thomas like many
others yielded to his charm. He wrote to Bishop
John Fisher: "I have come to court entirely against
my will, and as the king himself often jestingly re-

proaches me for. And I am as uncomfortable as a carpet knight in the saddle. . . Yet such is the virtue and learning of the king, and his daily increasing progress in both, that the more I see him increase in these kingly ornaments, the less troublesome the courtier's life becomes to me."

His son-in-law, Roper, the husband of Margaret, has given a vivid account of More's friendship with the king : The king used "upon holy days, when he had done his own devotions, to send for him into his traverse, and there — sometimes in matters of astronomy, geometry, divinity, and such other faculties, and sometimes of his worldly affairs — to sit and confer with him. And other whiles, in the night, would he have him up into the leads, there to consider with him the diversities, courses, motions, and operations of the stars and planets. And because he was of a pleasant disposition, it pleased the king and queen, after the council had supped, at the time of their supper, for their pleasure commonly to call for him to be merry with them. When he perceived them so much in his talk to delight, that he could not once in a month get leave to go home to his wife and children (whose company he most desired), and to be absent from the court two days together but that he should be thither sent for again : he, much misliking this restraint of his liberty, began there-

[174]

upon somewhat to dissemble his nature, and . . . by little and little, from his former mirth to disuse himself. . .

"And for the pleasure he took in his company would his grace suddenly sometimes come home to his house at Chelsea to be merry with him, whither, on a time, unlooked for, he came to dinner, and after dinner, in a fair garden of his, walked with him."

Roper, watching them from his window, noticed that for a whole hour of intimate conversation, the king, who was the taller of the two, walked with his arm thrown over More's shoulders.

"As soon as his grace was gone, I, rejoicing thereat, said to Sir Thomas More, how happy he was whom the king so familiarly entertained, as I never had seen him do to any before, except Cardinal Wolsey, whom I saw his grace walk once with arm in arm. 'I thank our Lord, son,' quoth he, 'I find his grace my very good lord indeed, and I believe he doth as singularly favor me as any subject within this realm : howbeit, son Roper, I may tell thee, I have no cause to be proud thereof, for if my head would win him a castle in France (for then there was war between us), it should not fail to go.'"

In his youth he had thought of studying for the priesthood, and of joining the Franciscans ; but on the advice of his confessor, Dean Colet, he gave up all idea of a religious vocation. Some of his biographers have hinted that he chose matrimony as an escape from a life of profligacy. Like most young men, he doubtless experienced the temptations of the flesh ; how far he may have yielded to them is a matter that concerns him and his confessor. At any rate he came to the conclusion that marriage was his vocation.

In 1505, he married Jane Colt, and five years of happiness followed. It was said that he preferred her younger sister, but when he realized that it might bring grief and shame to the elder sister to see the younger preferred before her, he then, "of a certain pity, framed his fancy toward her, and soon after married her." She bore him four children, Margaret, Elizabeth, Cecily and John. In the evenings after the children were asleep, the mother used to spend an hour or two in study, for her husband wished her to be a scholar ; or she would sing and play the clavichord, and as More delighted in music, she soon became a skilful amateur.

In 1510, very soon after the death of his first wife, he married Alice Middleton, who was some years older than himself. Following is an unconscious eulogy of her by Erasmus, although he wrote the passage in praise of his friend More :

A few months after his wife's death, he married a widow, who might take care of his children (the eldest, Margaret, was barely five) ; she was neither young nor fair, as he would say laughingly, but an active and vigilant housewife, with whom he lived as pleasantly and sweetly as if she had all the charms of youth. You will scarcely find a husband who, by authority or severity, has gained such ready compliance as More by playful flattery. What, indeed, would he not obtain, when he has prevailed on a woman already getting old, by no means of a pliable disposition, and intent on domestic affairs, to learn to play the harp, the lute, the monochord, and the flute, and, by the appointment of her husband, to devote to this task a fixed time every day ?

She was not a learned woman, and paid no more attention to the philosophical discussions which More carried on with Erasmus and his friends than a mother to the prattle of her children ; but she was favored with a sense of humor. In a letter to Erasmus of Dec. 15, 1517, More says : "My wife desires a million of compliments, especially for your careful wish that she may live many years. She says she is the more anxious for this as she will live the longer to plague me."

On one occasion after she had been to confession, she bade her husband be merry, "for I have," said she, "this day left all my shrewdness, and tomorrow I will begin afresh."

Harpsfield, Archdeacon of Canterbury under

Mary, tells of a good-natured rebuke More administered to his wife for her vanity: "When he divers times beheld his wife what pains she took in straight binding up her hair to make her a fair large forehead, and with straight bracing in her body to make her middle small, both twain to her great pain, for the pride of a little foolish praise, he said to her: 'Forsooth, madam, if God give you not hell, he shall do you great wrong, for it must needs be your own of very right, for you buy it very dear, and take very great pains therefor.'"

She, on the other hand, often reproached her husband for his lack of worldly ambition.

"What will you do," she asked, "that ye list not to put forth yourself as other folks do? Will you sit still by the fire, and make goslings in the ashes with a stick, as children do? Would God I were a man, and look what I would do."

"Why, wife," he replied, "what would you do?"

"What? by God, go forward with the best. For, as my mother was wont to say (God have mercy on her soul!) it is ever better to rule than to be ruled. And therefore, by God, I would not, I warrant you, be so foolish to be ruled when I might rule."

But More had the last word: "By my tooth, wife, in this I daresay you say truth, for I never found you willing to be ruled as yet."

The dominant interests in his home life were his children, and their education. Outside of his religion, his love for Margaret was the strongest passion of his life. Even after the children were married, they continued to live with their father to the end, and with his help and guidance brought up their own children.

More also loved his fool, Henry Patenson, and treated him as one of the family. In his *Utopia*, he writes, "They have a singular delight and pleasure in fools. And as it is a great reproach to do any of them hurt or injury, so they prohibit not to take pleasure of foolishness. For that, they think, doth much good to the fools. But if any man be so sad and stern that he cannot laugh, neither at their words nor at their deeds, none of them be committed to his tuition."

The home at Chelsea must have been something of a menagerie. According to Erasmus, "One of his great delights is to consider the forms, the habits, and the instincts of different kinds of animals. There is hardly a species of bird that he does not keep in his house, and rare animals, such as monkeys, foxes, ferrets, weasels, and the like. If he meets with anything foreign or in any way remarkable, he eagerly buys it, so that his house is full of such things, and at every turn they attract the eyes

of visitors, and his own pleasure is renewed whenever he sees others pleased."

II

IN spite of his wife's complaint that he lacked ambition, Thomas More's rise in public life was extremely rapid.   Having become a renowned lawyer,
he was elected to Parliament in 1504, when only
twenty-two.   In 1510 he was appointed Under-
sheriff of London, in 1518 Secretary to Henry VIII,
and in 1521 he was knighted.   He was chosen
Speaker of Parliament in 1523, and in 1529 he became Lord Chancellor of England in succession to
Cardinal Wolsey.

Notwithstanding the increasing demands made
upon his time by his official duties, he never ceased
his reading and study and writing.   It is as a scholar
rather than as a jurist that he is known to posterity.
All London knew that a man of intellect was at the
head of affairs ; but More himself had no illusions
as to what a philosopher in public office might accomplish.   He said in his *Utopia*, that "philosophy
had no place among kings," and declared that "it is
not possible for all things to be well, unless all men
were good, which I think will not be this good many
years."

[180]

SAINT THOMAS MORE

It was not merely because he preferred to be at home among his friends and family and books, that life at court was repugnant to him. The utter unreality and falsity of the courtiers and ladies palled upon him. Dice and cards were their constant amusement and occupation, and he regarded such things as a criminal waste of time. He had a horror of luxury and worldly pomp, and the idle and pampered life of those who surrounded the king annoyed him extremely. In his *Utopia*, ornaments of precious metals were worn only by criminals as a mark of their infamy. We can imagine what his thought must have been as he placed round his neck the heavy gold chain of the Chancellor.

Since her residence in France, Anne Boleyn had cultivated foreign ways and manners ; but More preferred the healthy rudenesses of his own beloved England. The lies and flatteries which were the daily pabulum of the hangers-on at court were nauseating to a man of his rugged sincerity.

Because of his English love of independence, it wearied him to be constantly at the king's command. Nevertheless we must not infer that it was self-indulgence or love of ease that made him prefer the life of a scholar. The reason was that he considered a scholar's life to be conducive to a virtuous life of piety toward God and service of his neighbor.

Virtue and religion were the supreme concerns of his life.

The following portion from a letter which he wrote to Gunnell, the tutor of his children, shows that he considered pride to be the chief danger of education :

The more I see the difficulty of getting rid of this pest of pride, the more do I see the necessity of setting to work at it from childhood. For I find no other reason why this evil clings so to our hearts, than because almost as soon as we are born it is sown in the tender minds of children by their nurses, it is cultivated by their teachers, and brought to its full growth by their parents. . . Thus we grow accustomed to make so much of praise, that while we study how to please the greater number (who will always be the worst), we grow ashamed of being good (with the few). That this plague of vainglory may be banished far from my children I do desire that you, my dear Gunnell, and their mother and all their friends, would sing this song to them, and repeat it, and beat it into their heads, that vainglory is a thing despicable and to be spit upon ; and that there is nothing more sublime than that humble modesty so often praised by Christ.

The real Thomas More is revealed in this letter. To his mind, the end of education was virtue. It should inculcate a spirit of detachment from riches and earthly possessions, along with a spirit of gentleness. The controlling aim in all his manifold activities was perfection. Truth, reality, justice — in his estimation — far outweighed social popularity, worldly honor and monetary reward.

He has been blamed for being too lenient in his judgments as Chancellor. His heart overflowed with charity for the criminal, and he believed that the penalties laid down by the law were entirely out of proportion to the gravity of the crimes. Theft was a felony punishable with death and the confiscation of all the goods of the offender. In the reign of Henry VIII, some 12,000 human beings were put to death for this crime alone.

Contrary to the common opinion among non-Catholics that he was merciless in his treatment of heretics, he shrank from applying the death penalty. If he could not dissuade them from their heresy himself, he sent them to their bishop in the hope that they might thereby be won back to the faith. Although no one believed more strongly than he that heresy was a grievous social crime, yet it was not until the last months of his administration that he condemned any to death for heresy ; even then he was responsible for only four executions.

III

Sir Thomas More was a leader of the humanists, an ardent champion of the study of the Greek and

Latin classics, sympathetic with most of the tendencies of the Renaissance, and along with his friend Erasmus, an advocate of many needed reforms in the Church; yet he was firmly grounded in the Catholic tradition of the Middle Ages, and nothing could budge him from his position.

Some Catholics have been shocked by More's friendship with Erasmus, "the forerunner of the Reformation," and insist that it meant that More was growing lax in his devotion to the Catholic Church. It meant nothing of the kind. Nor did their friendship grow lukewarm. More was intensely fond of Erasmus till the end, which could not have been true if Erasmus had weakened in his loyalty to Catholicism. It is true that Erasmus in his *Praise of Folly* had written some witty epigrams against the monks, and had somewhat harshly rebuked certain superstitious devotions. It was written in 1508, but its satire was moderate compared with that of many who had written before that date on the need of reform in the Church.

In 1527, Erasmus wrote in a letter : "I wrote the *Praise of Folly* in times of peace ; I should never have written it if I had foreseen this tempest." Writing later to a monk who wished to leave his monastery, he said :

I fear that you are imposed upon by the trickery of certain people who nowadays go boasting mightily of the liberty of the gospel. Believe me, if you knew more of things, you would be less weary of your present life. I see a race of men arising from whom my mind turns with loathing. I see no one becoming better, every one becoming worse, so that I am deeply grieved that in my writings I once preached the liberty of the spirit, though I did so in all honesty, suspecting nothing so little as the appearance of people of this kind. What I desired then was that the abatement of external ceremonies might much redound to the increase of true piety. But as it is, the ceremonies have been so destroyed that in place of them we have not the liberty of the spirit but the unbridled license of the flesh. . . What liberty is that which forbids us to say our prayers, and forbids us the sacrifice of the Mass?

It is chiefly through his *Utopia* that Sir Thomas More is known to every school-boy today. It is one of the classics of English literature. Yet, strangely enough, it was written in Latin, and was never intended by its author for general circulation. He did not think it could safely be read by the multitude. He wrote it as a *jeu d'esprit*, and entrusted the manuscript only to his special friends. They received it in the proper spirit, as a satire on the contemporary world, for in *Utopia* More drew a picture in which everything was the exact opposite of what was found in the England and Europe of 1516. If we bear that contrast in mind as we read the *Utopia*, we can guess what were his real thoughts regarding the civilization and manners of his time.

Why was this saintly and brilliant humanist, this intimate companion of the king, this Chancellor beloved of all the people of England, this master of witty epigrams, this man of letters with an European reputation, imprisoned in the Tower and finally beheaded? He was hardly the sort of man whom the world would have marked out for martyrdom. Not even the most worldly-minded would call him an obstreperous fanatic or an intolerant dogmatist.

Sir Thomas More would not move his little finger to enable Henry to put away his wife, and to supplant the Pope as supreme head of the Church in England; therefore he went to the block. That was of small moment to him; for, as he often said, "A man may very well lose his head and yet come to no harm."

Sir Thomas More and Bishop John Fisher were two of the noblest men England ever produced. The Emperor Charles the Fifth said that had he been the fortunate possessor of two such faithful counsellors, he would rather have lost the strongest city in his wide dominions than suffer himself to be deprived of them. They were sent to the Tower in 1534 for refusing to take the Oath of Succession, which would have obligated them to accept as successors to the Crown the children of Anne Boleyn. We do not know on what grounds More refused the Oath, but it is probable that when the Oath was administered it included a sentence declaring Henry's marriage to Catherine invalid. Both More and Fisher were willing to swear allegiance to any heir to the throne whom the king and Parliament might agree upon, but that did not satisfy Anne Boleyn.

When More had been in prison a month, his wife, who had visited him faithfully and ministered to his needs, finally lost patience with him and rebuked him for his foolish obstinacy in holding out against the royal demands. She asked him why he could not do as other men did, when it would deliver him from that filthy cell and enable him to return to his family and books at Chelsea.

He met her query with another: "Don't you think, Mistress Alice, that this place is as near to heaven as Chelsea?"

As he pressed her for an answer, she would only say, "Tilly vally"!

Then more seriously he asked, "Suppose I were to go back to my house in Chelsea, how long do you think we would live to enjoy it?"

"Possibly twenty years," she replied.

"Twenty years!" said he. "Why, if you had said a thousand years it would have been something, and

[187]

yet it would be a very bad merchant that would put himself into danger to lose eternity for a thousand years ; how much the rather as we are not sure of it for one day ?"

In a few weeks the servile Parliament passed the Act of Supremacy, which made it high treason to refuse to accept the king as "the only supreme head in earth of the Church of England." When questioned by messengers from the king, More refused to commit himself as to what he thought of this new Act. He would not act presumptuously. He wrote in a letter to Margaret : "I have not been a man of such holy living, as I might be bold to offer myself to death, lest God for my presumption might suffer me to fall ; therefore I put not myself forward but draw back. Howbeit, if God draw me to it himself, then trust I in his great mercy, that he shall not fail to give me grace and strength."

When he was brought to trial on the perjured evidence of Richard Rich, he skilfully defended himself against the unjust charge that he had spoken against the Act of Supremacy. He said to the judges : "If I were a man, my lords, that did not regard an oath, I need not stand in this place, at this time, as an accused person. And if this oath of yours, Mr. Rich, be true, then I pray that I may never see the face of God, which I would not say were it otherwise to win the whole world." He added, "In good faith, Mr. Rich, I am sorrier for your perjury than for my own peril."

The rest of the trial was a mockery of justice. More was convicted of high treason for having spoken against the royal supremacy over the Church. Lord Campbell, in his *Lives of the Chancellors*, gives this well-considered judgment: "We must regard the murder of Sir Thomas More as the blackest crime that has ever been perpetrated in England under the form of law."

"It is not death, but the cause of death, which makes the martyr." Blessed Thomas More was a martyr, because of his steadfast defence of two fundamental principles of the Catholic religion: the indissolubility of marriage and the supremacy of the Pope. In protest against cutting off the Church of England from Rome, the centre of unity, he was willing to lay down his life.

After the sentence of death was pronounced, he saw no further reason for silence and definitely proclaimed his reasoned conviction: "Forasmuch as, my Lords, this indictment is grounded upon an Act of Parliament, directly oppugnant to the laws of God and his Holy Church, the supreme government of which, or of any part thereof, may no temporal prince presume by any law to take upon him, as rightfully belonging to the see of Rome, a spiritual pre-eminence by the mouth of our Saviour himself, personally present upon the earth, to Saint Peter and his successors, bishops of the same see, by special prerogative granted, it is therefore in law amongst Christian men insufficient to charge any Christian."

He had prepared a long statement to make on the scaffold, but as the king requested that his words be few on that occasion, he did not read it. Among the few words he did utter, one sentence expressed concisely the dominant aim of his whole life : "I have been ever the king's good and loyal servant, but God's first."

He was a man of broad culture and versatile interests ; a faithful husband and devoted father ; the best talker in England and a loyal friend ; a gifted man of letters and one of the most eminent classical scholars of his time ; a brilliant lawyer and a just Chancellor ; a diplomat and a statesman ; a theologian and an ascetic ; a satirist on ecclesiastical abuses and an indefatigable champion of the Church and the Papacy : but God always came first, the eternal was always preferred to the temporal.

Because he loved God above all things, he could joke on his way to the scaffold. His last words were the well-known jest about his beard, which during his imprisonment had been allowed to grow. With his head on the block, he said to the executioner: "Wait till I put aside my beard, for *that* never committed treason."

MADAME ACARIE

BLESSED MARIE OF THE INCARNATION
[1566-1618]

THE lives of the saints often make humorous reading. This is not so much because many of them were generously endowed with the sense of humor, but because of the extraordinary interventions of Providence in fashioning their careers. It is amusing to see how Almighty God will insist on getting things done His way, although all sorts of important individuals — who have not the slightest intention of coöperating with Him — are bent on frustrating His designs. They blunder along in their pride and stubborn self-will, and all unknown to them God is using them to carry out His purposes.

This was notably the case with Madame Acarie. God caused her to be born in France at that particular time because He wanted a definite work to be done. Her mother, her husband, her doctors, even some of the clergy, attempted to put obstacles in the way ; but God either brushed them aside or made them do His bidding in spite of themselves. They contributed to the development of a saint and prepared the ground for the work which God sent that saint into the world to accomplish.

We often wonder why God does not intervene more in the affairs of our troubled world. Perhaps He would, if there were more men and women who responded to their vocation to be saints. It is primarily through those generous souls who have surrendered themselves to His will that the Creator and Ruler of all things conveys His blessings to the world. The saints are the levers employed by the Almighty to lift humanity to better things.

I

BARBE AVRILLOT was born in Paris in 1566 of well-bred parents. Her father, in manner somewhat stiff and repelling, was a good Catholic, and after the death of his wife became a priest. He had been associated with the *Ligue* which fought against Henry of Navarre, and when he came to the throne as Henry IV, M. Avrillot lost his property. Barbe's mother was often harsh and violent toward her, and she became a timid and frightened child. She was no doubt glad to leave such a gloomy home to be educated in a convent of strict observance.

She wanted to become a nun, but her mother

would not hear of it. She asked permission to become a nursing sister, but again her mother refused, and insisted on her marrying. The mother had chosen a husband for her, M. Pierre Acarie, who had been a King's Councillor but was exiled after the victory of Henry of Navarre; and they were married when Barbe was a little over sixteen.

Pierre Acarie was a hot-headed, fantastic adventurer, with little worldly common sense. He was indolent and critical at home, given to teasing his wife, and passed quickly from coarse laughter to uncontrolled anger. The Jesuit Père Commolet was the only one who could persuade him to recede from unreasonable decisions. For instance, he flatly refused to allow his wife to go to Pontoise on business connected with a newly founded monastery. Père de Berulle interceded for her with Père Commolet, and he obtained the desired permission from the stubborn husband.

M. Acarie conceived it to be his duty to censor his wife's reading. One day he went into a rage when he found her reading a new romance, *Amadis*, and absolutely forbade her to read romances of any kind. He said he would ask his confessor to lend him a supply of the kind of books she ought to read. A few days later the timid young wife found on her desk a pile of books on the spiritual life, which she

proceeded dutifully to read. These books introduced her to a new world of mystical reality of which
up to that time she knew nothing. Entranced by its
infinite expanses of beauty and glory, she felt that
the sense world no longer had anything to give her.

One sentence in one of these books made a lasting
impression on her soul :

Trop est avare à qui Dieu ne suffit.
[Too greedy is he for whom God does not suffice].

These words transformed her whole being, and
she was then only twenty-two. They seemed to
give her a new heart, a new soul, a new understanding. Her gait was altered, her hearing and seeing ;
and a changed tone was noticed in her voice. She
lost her timidity and became more decisive and effi-
cient in the management of her household. Her
husband perceived the change but did not understand what had come over her. Perhaps he had
suspicions that she had fallen in love with someone
else, as indeed she had.

II

Of all the husbands who have attempted to dictate
what their wives should read, Pierre Acarie deserves
the palm. The results, both immediate and ulti-

mate, were astounding. Madame Acarie attained at once to the higher reaches of contemplative prayer. So intense was her concentration, and so absorbed did she become in what she saw and heard in her prayer, that she often fell into ecstasy. The crises were sometimes awkward. One day she had an ecstasy after receiving Holy Communion, and remained kneeling in church oblivious of the passing hours. As she had not returned home when evening came on, the family became anxious and sent to the church to make inquiries. She was found still on her knees, and when someone touched her, she looked up surprised and asked if the Mass was over.

On another occasion it happened when she was talking with her mother-in-law — possibly the highest compliment that has ever been paid by a wife to her mother-in-law. This good lady went about repeating to her friends: "What ails my daughter? I do not know her; my satisfaction with her has not lasted long."

These ecstatic states seemed to have no bad effect on her health and did not waste her strength. According to her biographer, who was for a time her confessor, M. Duval, "far from these austerities and violent seizures wasting her strength, she daily became fatter and more highly colored."

Neither did they interfere with her bearing of children. They came rapidly from her twenty-second year on — both the ecstasies and the children. Three had been born before the ecstasies began : in 1584, 1585 and 1587. Three more were to come, in 1589, 1590 and 1592. All were healthy children, three boys and three girls.

Though she was never really ill, the doctors whom her worried husband consulted concluded that as her complexion was more rosy when she came out of the ecstasies she must have too much blood, so they ordered her to be bled. For three years at least even her confessors did not know what to think of the continual ecstasies and ravishments which befell her.

Finally the chief mystical authority in Paris was consulted, the Père Benedict of Canfeld, an English Capuchin, and he relieved the family temporarily by assuring them, "All comes from God ; she must yield herself to the Divine working."

One effect of this tendency to ecstatic states was that Madame Acarie found it impossible to read spiritual and mystical books without immediately falling into ecstasy. Therefore she had someone read them to her. The presence of another person usually kept her on the natural plane. When alone she often played the spinet to distract herself from contemplation. However as she advanced toward perfection, she gained better control over her inner life, and the ecstatic seizures became more infrequent.

The French Jesuit, Père de Grandmaison, in his book on *Personal Religion,* makes some illuminating remarks on this point :

We must beware of sharing the popular belief that these ecstatic phenomena constitute the essential part of the mystic state and call for admiration ; they are but the concomitants, the consequences, the price thereof. They are due to the weakness and imperfection, the insufficient spiritualization of the human instrument, and they diminish with its progress. Ecstasy, I use the term strictly for the phenomena of inhibition, temporary unconsciousness, is neither an honor nor a virtue ; it is a tribute paid by the mystics to their human nature. It is also to be remembered that it can be imitated, or, perhaps I may rather say, produced by all kinds of causes.

Madame Acarie also received the stigmata in her hands and feet, although it was known only to her most intimate associates. She concealed her hands as much as possible ; and as she had three times broken her ankles and in her later years walked on crutches, few people knew of the infirmity in her feet.

Her mystical life was of a passive character rather than active. God seemed to seize possession of her soul without any effort on her part. Vocal prayer, like devotional reading, was extremely difficult for her. Her approach to God in contemplation was *per modum fulguris coruscantis,* and her countenance became luminous, like the face of Moses on the mount. Whenever she was interrupted in conversation, she concentrated so eagerly on God that she forgot what she had been saying. She would often say, "Let us talk of that"—and then could not complete her sentence.

She was very reserved about her mystical illuminations. Her profound humility is evident from the following incident as reported by Duval:

A religious once said some words to her regarding the sublimity of her devotion. She replied promptly : "Father, I should be well content if I could live in the fear of God, and the keeping of His commandments, capable of telling my beads properly. What more can a married woman do with a household and children to manage ?"

III

PIERRE ACARIE, somewhat chagrined perhaps at the spiritual progress of his wife and her growing renown as a mystic, began to apply himself to the study of books of piety. He even went to the expense of having some of the writings of the Blessed

Angela of Foligno translated into French and presenting them to his wife. One sympathises with his hurt feelings when she refused to read them on the ground that they distracted her from her inner life and hindered rather than helped the Divine operations in her soul.

One does not sympathise with the actions to which his hurt pride then led him. He began to make life uncomfortable for her at home, and went so far as to malign her to the priests as a hysterical woman puffed up with pride by her dangerous illusions. They believed him because he had a reputation for truthfulness, and because, as the Abbé Brémond remarks, "many priests are always ready to believe anything said against the mystics." One Sunday he took his whole household, including the servants, to hear a preacher, whom he had already primed with false stories, hold up to scorn the kind of woman whose ecstatic devotions led her to neglect her duties in her home. When some of the servants asked Madame Acarie what she thought of the sermon, she laughed and said it would soon be forgotten. On another occasion a priest deliberately passed her over in administering Holy Communion, but she acted as if she did not notice it.

The truth is that she never neglected her household duties because of her religious practices. She often left the church immediately after receiving Holy Communion, in order that she might attend to her husband's breakfast. She may have been unduly conscientious in trying to protect the servants from his too great familiarity with them, but otherwise she let him go his own way. By his reckless expenditures he was speedily reducing his wife and six children to poverty. He was no doubt a man of good intentions, but weak in his mental processes. He therefore was an easy prey to sharpers with their get-rich-quick schemes.

For political reasons M. Acarie spent four years in exile. Henry IV, out of his high esteem for Madame Acarie, made these years as comfortable as possible for her husband. These four years of independence were utilized by Madame Acarie in her efforts to save her house and rehabilitate her husband's reputation. She displayed unusual business and legal acumen. It would take too long to explain the financial disgrace in which he had become implicated ; but during these years of freedom his wife mastered the case, drew up the brief in his defense and herself acted as the attorney before the court. She was rewarded by his complete exoneration.

If her husband would not have acclaimed her the ideal wife, her children would certainly have agreed that she was the ideal mother. She took deep interest in their education and especially in the training of their characters. She overlooked many of their shortcomings but she hated lies, and never failed to punish for the sin of falsehood. Duval records her saying to her daughters who were taller than she : "If you were as tall as the rafters, I would hire women to hold you down."

She believed in the efficacy of the rod, but never used it at the moment of the offense when her children were in a passion. She also did her best to combat vanity in her children. She would not permit the servants to use the title *Mademoiselle* in addressing her daughters, but only their Christian names ; and she insisted on their saying "Pray" or "Please" when asking anything of the servants. As another means of making them humble, she imposed acts of humiliation and mortification by way of punishment, as when she made her eldest daughter sweep the stairs in front of guests.

She said she would never be guilty of the crime of driving her daughters into a convent ; and if they went they must go of their own free-will. For this reason she taught them to carry themselves well and dress neatly and attractively according to the fashion. She would not have it said that they entered religion because no one would marry them. She said, "I do not wish any physical excuse to serve as a motive for such a step."

Her three daughters did subsequently become Carmelites and two of her sons became priests. Her wisdom in the training of her children, as well as in her many works of apostolic charity, was the direct outcome of her inner mystical experiences. The grace which she drew from contemplation directed and guided her in all her manifold beneficent activities. This becomes evident from the following comment by M. Duval :

Assuredly her soul was enlightened by some special ray of the Divine, bestowing on her unerring judgment in things earthly as well as heavenly. In good truth she once was favored by God with a marvellous glimpse of His Providence over men, which lasted for three days, during which she saw, heard or thought of nought but the incomprehensible way in which God governs all things . . . (and as this Divine governing embraces all things) we saw her advising on highly spiritual matters, and immediately afterwards abasing herself to direct bodily exigencies and temporal affairs.

The second daughter, Marguerite du Saint-Sacrement, as she was known in religion, is regarded by the Abbé Brémond as the ideal Carmelite. She was direct, brisk and simple in speech, and gave the impression to outsiders of being almost silly. She even

took in her mother, who said that she was afraid that
her daughter's inner life must be in a deplorable
condition. Nevertheless she once asked her daughter — then a Carmelite — for criticism as to her own
spiritual state. Marguerite du Saint-Sacrement replied without hesitation :

"You must mortify self, for, though you have
taught others so much, you have always followed
your own inclinations, and, good though they are,
there is too much of your own judgment in your
actions, and that is what you must let die within you."

Madame Acarie told some sisters of this advice,
and they later expressed their surprise to Sister Marguerite, saying with a smile, "What behaviour !"

"Then why did she ask me," she replied, "when
she knows me to be nothing but a giddy ass ! I
could not say anything else but what I thought."[1]

IV

M. GAUTHIER, Councillor of State, and an intimate
friend of Madame Acarie, testified on oath during
the process for her canonization that she was responsible for at least 10,000 conversions. The King,
Henry IV, said that he valued her good opinion as

[1] Henri Brémond, *A Literary History of Religious Thought in France*,
English translation, vol. II, p. 253. I am indebted to his study of
Madame Acarie for most of my facts.

highly as that of anyone in Paris. She had the faculty of awakening seriousness of mind in all who approached her. Duval tells us that "she never willingly applied herself to any mundane business without first perceiving an inward prompting thereto." That is the secret apparently of her extraordinary influence over her contemporaries. All who approached her were impressed by her genuine spirituality, and felt that in talking with her they were coming very close to God Himself.

The Abbé Brémond remarks that she "liberated grace" in countless men and women, including many priests. His explanation of this phenomenon is worth noting :

Mysticism is, after all, but Christian seriousness raised to the highest degree. God alone makes the saint and the mystic, but His call to those whom He has chosen is sometimes almost imperceptible. Many do not hear it or dare not hear it ; whether from weakness or ill-conceived humility or prudence, they paralyze, they stifle grace. But — and this is the great Divine Law ruling most supernatural ascents,— the words, or it may be no more than the sight, of a soul truly holy and manifestly possessed of God, reveal their own latent gift to these timid, hesitating elect who do not "know themselves."

While M. Acarie was in exile, his wife inspired a number of secular ladies who often gathered at her home, to form the *Congrégation de Sainte-Gene-*

viève, to enable them to live a holy life in common and instruct little girls. At first they wore hoods, but as the hoods were so becoming that they became the fashion among the smart ladies of Paris, Madame Acarie dissuaded them from wearing any distinctive garb. This Congregation prepared the ground for the founding of Carmelite and Ursuline houses in France, as most of its members joined these two new orders.

Not only did Madame Acarie prepare the way for the introduction of the Carmelite order into France, but she was directly responsible for initiating the delicate negotiations with the Spanish branch, so recently reformed by Saint Teresa, which would effect the transfer. She was led to take this step not by reading the Life of Saint Teresa which had been translated into French — as when it was read to her she was not deeply stirred — but by a vision of Saint Teresa herself, who commanded her to confer with the proper authorities whose consent must first be obtained. She called a meeting of Cardinal Bérulle and other influential priests, but they concluded that the moment was not propitious for any kind of an invasion from Spain. Saint Teresa again appeared to Madame Acarie, urging her to proceed without delay, as the way would be made clear. She immediately summoned her group again, and Saint

Francis of Sales, who was then preaching in Paris, joined them. The result of their deliberations was that the first French Carmel was founded in Paris in 1606. During the next nine years six more foundations were made in Amiens, Tours, Rouen, Bordeaux, Besançon and Dieppe.

While still living with her husband, Madame Acarie selected and trained many young women who afterwards became Carmelites. She possessed the gift of discernment of spirits to an unusual degree. Many of those whom she trained became founders of convents. She was given a free hand in this work by Henri de Gondi, Archbishop of Paris ; and had the assistance and counsel of Cardinal de Bérulle. Carmelite superiors also did not hesitate to make use of her. On this point M. Duval is interesting : "Though ordinarily women religious do not willingly defer to married women, at least in matters regarding their interior life, yet God had bestowed upon her for that purpose such special graces, and she behaved with such humility and tact, that they made no difficulty in opening their hearts to her wholly and declaring their inmost thoughts to her."

While occupied with this work of testing candidates, her house became a center of religious activity. Her husband often became a troublesome interloper, even going so far as to read some of the letters addressed by aristocratic young women to his wife. He was quite frank in giving expression to his irritation, as when he said, "It is uncommonly inconvenient to have such a saintly wife and one so skilled in giving advice."

However, he received some consolation in being permitted to entertain charming young ladies while they were waiting for an appointment to discuss their vocation with his wife. One of them took him for a drive and made herself so agreeable that he remarked to his wife that it was criminal for such a young woman to become a nun. She afterwards became a mother superior.

Madame Acarie rejected many candidates who were strongly recommended to her. Of one such aspirant she said:

"If it depended on me, I should not for all the world receive her. She is one of those characters who, by prudence and complaisance, not by grace, avoid committing faults."

She dismissed another young woman with this comment: "The girl is not frank; her lips are not in agreement with her heart."

Her reasons for refusing to accept a wealthy young widow were indicated when she said: "I trouble myself not at all about the money needed for the material building, but solely about the living stones which shall build up the spiritual edifice. Did I know of a soul fitted for this last, I should be ready to give all the gold of the universe to buy it ; or to give as much to exclude one not fitted."

She once said of a priest who, she thought, was too easy in testing vocations : "One must search the depths of the heart and see whether God is there, or at least whether He will be there, when the soul is prepared by religion."

That was her supreme test of the reality of one's spiritual life — "whether God is there." The saying of Our Lord that was most frequently upon her lips was, "The kingdom of God is within you." We are reminded again of that sentence from a mystical writer that changed the whole current of her life : "Too greedy is he for whom God does not suffice !"

Saint Francis de Sales, like many others, felt the spell of her sanctity. He wrote of her :

She was an eminent servant of God, and I heard her confession many times, almost regularly for six months (in 1602), and notably in her illnesses of that time. Oh, what a loss was mine, not to have profited by her holy conversation, for she would willingly have communicated her whole soul to me, but the infinite respect I had for her held me back from questioning her.

M. Pierre Acarie died in 1613. Soon afterwards his widow joined the Carmelites, but only as a lay sister, taking the name *Marie of the Incarnation*. She lived first in the convent at Amiens, but later was transferred to Pontoise, where she died in 1618. She was beatified in 1791.

M. Duval, her confessor for many years and her biographer, was also a learned Doctor of the Sorbonne. He saw his former penitent for the last time when she was leaving the convent in Amiens, where she had been professed, for Pontoise. His description of the scene is memorable:

Passing through the cloisters at first I did not see Sister Marie of the Incarnation, who was at the foot of the steps leading to the cloisters, because I was examining the stained glass in which was depicted the life of the Blessed Mother Teresa. He who accompanied me, however, drew my attention to her. I turned round, but did not at first recognize her, so radiant and absolutely dazzling did her face appear to me. Although I had seen her a million times in the world, I nevertheless said to my informant: "I should never have recognized her if you had not told me." I had never before seen her thus; and this view of her has remained so strongly imprinted on my mind that I never think of her without forthwith beholding that scene in the cloister at Amiens.

BLESSED ANNA MARIA TAIGI
[1769-1837]

MANY wives and mothers today are living as holy a life as Blessed Anna Maria Taigi, the Roman workingman's wife who became an expert in washing and darning clothes, as well as fine sewing and cooking; but it is doubtful whether their piety and sufferings will make them equally famous. Anna Maria's holy life attracted wide attention because she was also something of a fortune teller — what indeed in secular circles today would probably be called a crystal gazer. She was consulted by queens, princes, cardinals and popes. Nowadays we have laundresses and seamstresses who are holy, but few of them can foretell the future; and our fortune tellers are not often saints.

I

ANNA MARIA GIANETTI was born in Siena on May 29, 1769. Her father was a chemist; but he was soon reduced to poverty, and set out with his family for Rome to seek employment for himself and wife

as house servants. Anna Maria left school after
her confirmation when about thirteen, and learned
the trade of wool-winder, which she soon gave up
for a position as house-maid in a noble family.
When eighteen she married Domenico Taigi, who
was in service near by in the Chigi palace. Partly
to please him, partly to gratify her own vanity, she
began to dress more gaily and display her beauty
under the bright sun of Rome.

Soon after their marriage, a catastrophe occurred in
the life of the young bride, which is left out of most
of the accounts of her life. She fell into grave sin.
She was lured from the path of virtue by an older
man, who pursued her persistently until she yielded
to him. It was but a momentary lapse ; nevertheless her conscience tormented her. When with her
husband she was overwhelmed with shame and remorse. For some months she sought consolation in
the distractions of a worldly life, but these distractions brought her no peace. This painful experience
throws light on the severe penitential discipline in
her later years.

Not long after this she had an experience which
completely changed the course of her life. One
holiday afternoon, she was tripping gaily with her
husband across the Piazza of Saint Peter's. They
passed one of the Servite Fathers, Padre Angelo,

who gave her a piercing look, which seemed to her like a warning of some impending judgment. It is said that he had received a revelation from God that a certain woman would come to him to be directed into the way of sanctity, and when he passed Anna Maria he knew she was the one whom God had chosen. Be that as it may, it is undeniable that the first impulse to conversion has often come from a glance of the eyes or an expression on the face of one who is living a holy life.

She hastened to the high altar over the tomb of Saint Peter, and fell on her knees. Conscious of her need of forgiveness, she sought out a confessional. For some unknown reason the priest sent her away, telling her she was not one of his usual penitents.

Some days later she was accidentally led into Padre Angelo's confessional. He greeted her with these words : "So you have come at last ! Be of good cheer, my child ; God loves you and he asks for your whole heart in return."

This was the decisive hour of her conversion — not from a life wholly given to sin, but from a life partly given to the world to one completely surrendered to God.

An immense joy took possession of her. She had an impulse to enter a convent ; but she concluded that married life was her vocation, and that if such was God's will for her, she could serve him only there. From that day forward, with her husband's consent, she put away her trinkets and necklaces and bright colors, and became a Tertiary of the Order of the Most Blessed Trinity.

On the day when she became a Tertiary, God entrusted this humble woman with an, almost superhuman task. After receiving Holy Communion, she heard the Saviour's voice saying to her :

"Know that I have chosen thee to convert sinners, and to console sufferers of every rank and station, priest and religious, even my Vicar himself. All who listen to thy words and carry out the commands transmitted through thee, shall receive great graces. Thou shalt meet with falsehood and perfidy, thou shall be mocked, despised, calumniated ; but thou wilt endure all this for love of Me."

Overcome with amazement, she asked, "O Lord, hast thou chosen *me* for such an office ? I am but a poor woman, unworthy to tread this earth."

"I have revealed my will to thee," was the answer, "I will lead thee by the hand as the shepherd leads the lamb to the altar of sacrifice, and all things shall be accomplished."

II

In fourteen years, Anna Maria Taigi gave birth to four sons and three daughters. Three of the children died when very young. Later on, one of the daughters was left a widow with six young children, and Anna Maria insisted on her bringing them all to live in the home of their grandparents. As Domenico Taigi earned only six crowns a month, the daughter asked how so many mouths could be fed on so slender an income.

Her mother replied : "Why do you worry ? Try to have more faith and trust God better. You know he has never failed to give me enough for myself and my children, and you may be sure he will do as much for you, and for the dear little ones whom he has entrusted to your care."

Anna Maria instructed her children in the elements of the Catholic religion, and tried to form their characters after the divine Model. She was strict with them and did not spare the rod. She never permitted them to go out unaccompanied, even to church or to school, except that the boys — after they were apprenticed — went to their work alone. She would hardly have permitted her girls to run through the streets alone to the market, like the little girls one sees today in the poorer quarters of Rome, with a loaf of bread and a bottle of wine under their arms.

The children had other things to remember their mother by beside discipline and hard work. On feast-days she would prepare for them a special dish, making use of left-over scraps brought home by her husband from the Palazzo Chigi. On Sundays after Mass she usually took them into the country for a picnic, or perhaps a pilgrimage to some famous shrine. After a visit to the church, they sat down under a shady tree for their feast of chestnuts and wine, followed by a siesta. Then they picked berries or wildflowers until they returned home in the evening.

Signora Taigi was in the habit of rising long before daybreak, and went to Mass daily. She often worked far into the night. By taking in sewing and washing she made enough to provide for the needs of her household with something left over for the poor. Her house was spotlessly clean and her children well-cared for. She would not allow them to accept a position which was morally dangerous or one which would take them out of their station of life. She rarely accepted financial help. When an exiled queen offered her money to make certain necessary purchases for the household, she refused to

accept it, saying, "Madame, how great is your simplicity! I serve Almighty God, and he is more
powerful than you!"

Domenico Taigi was not a saint. He was not a
bad husband, as husbands go; but he was only
moderately good. It rarely happens that both husband and wife are saints. Domenico was given to
fits of ill temper, which his wife met with kindly
words or no words at all. After her death he said,
"It is due to her that I corrected some of my faults."

He was often required to be at his work until two
or three in the morning; on returning home he found
his wife up and waiting for him. She was glad of
an excuse to spend the quiet hours in prayer. She
would do nothing without her husband's permission,
for she honored him as the head of the family.
Often on his return home he would find the house
full of visitors, but she would leave them to minister
to his needs.

In this crowded home, Anna Maria's parents spent
their last years, and they were difficult to get on with.
Her mother was often irritable, and had many sug-
gestions to offer about running the household. The
father was an invalid, and before his death was afflicted with loathesome sores which his daughter
bathed and dressed to the end. Domenico said in

his testimony after his wife's death, "It almost seems that God had given her such parents in order to try her virtue."

She was a good story-teller, and often entertained her children with interesting tales, many of which dealt with the lives of the saints. She was merry, easy to get on with and a good sort. Domenico bears witness on this point : "She spoke of God and holy things without becoming tiresome, not like some pious women who are always talking of themselves, and making a great parade of devotion. She would join in any conversation on ordinary subjects as long as there was no harm in it, and would laugh at our jokes ; but so great was her prudence that little by little the conversation took a pious turn, and we were caught before we were aware of it."

One day during the famine, Anna Maria's mother sent away from the door a starving beggar. Her daughter on hearing of it was much grieved, and exclaimed, "For God's sake, dear mother, never refuse an alms to any one. If there is nothing else, you will always find bread in this cupboard ; and you can give a bit to all who ask for it."

Domenico Taigi ends his deposition concerning the virtues of his beloved wife with these words : "I am not good at expressing myself, for I am old ; but if I were a young man, and could hunt the whole world over to find such another wife it would be vain. I believe that God has at last received her into his heaven because of her great virtue, and I hope that she will pray for me and for my family."

III

ANNA MARIA rarely sat down to eat at the table. She waited on her family and ate the fragments that remained on their plates. She fasted on Saturdays in honor of the Blessed Virgin, and on Wednesdays in honor of Saint Joseph. Although she ate little at any time, she practised still greater mortification on Fridays and kept rigorously the Lenten and Ember fasts. Sometimes her husband would command her to drink a glass of water, and she would obey. The motive of her austerities was not to keep thin and live long, but to mortify her self-love. She said once, "If we want to learn to love God, we must always row against the stream, and never cease to thwart our own will. The greedier the ass, the tighter we must hold the reins."

Humility and meekness were her favorite virtues. Humility led her to obey her confessor's directions, her husband, and other members of her family. She deliberately chose the lowest place, and rejoiced in humiliation and contempt. She sublimated to spir-

itual ends her natural love of submission and obedience. She loved those who hated and spoke ill of
her, and had many detractors. Caring nothing for
the favor of the rich she was oblivious to praise.
She spoke freely and fearlessly to distinguished
people, whenever she felt that God had given her a
word to say to them.

With humility went meekness and patience. She
often quoted the words of our Lord, "Learn of Me,
for I am meek and humble of heart."

He made this further revelation to her, "The
humble are always patient, and the patient sanctify
themselves. Patience is the best of all penances, and
he who is truly patient possesses all earthly treasure,
and will receive a heavenly crown."

In her case patience meant not only gentle forbearance toward her parents, husband and children;
but the uncomplaining acceptance of the trials of
poverty, unremitting toil and much physical suffering — to say nothing of frequent spiritual perplexity
and desolation. For forty-seven years she perse-
vered in her life of penitential discipline and vicarious suffering. Even at the end, when her family
left the room where she lay dying, she met death
alone, thus sharing in our Lord's agony of desolation.

Though her surroundings were ordinary, her mystical experiences were often of an extraordinary char-

acter : revelations, visions, rapture and ecstasies. It was not these experiences that made her a saint; it was rather because she was a saint that she had the experiences. She was a saint because she tried in everything to act in conformity with the will of God.

Her ecstasies sometimes came upon her at inconvenient moments, when she was in the midst of her housework. On one occasion at least she gave frank expression to her annoyance by saying, "O Lord, leave me in peace! Withdraw thyself and let me get on with my work. Keep the treasures of thy love for consecrated virgins; I am only a poor wife and mother."

Her visions came to her in an unusual way. Soon after her conversion, she saw before her a globe of dull gold, which gradually brightened into a ball of fire like a miniature sun. In this flaming disc she read the secrets of many hearts, the fate of departed souls, the past and future of individuals and nations. Through this means she could recognize people she had never seen. She knew the cause of people's misfortunes and could suggest remedies. She never made use of this revealed knowledge except when charity demanded it, or it might be for the glory of God. She often beheld mysterious apparitions which she did not venture to explain.

This symbolic sun, in which she saw many things

that were useful to souls, drew to the humble home of the Taigis innumerable visitors of every rank — rich and poor, princes and princesses, priests and cardinals. Three popes treated her with veneration, and listened to her counsels.

Her life was lived in disturbing times, when the rise of unbelief incident to the ferment of ideas before the French Revolution threatened the existence of the Church ; and the Pope, deceived by forged letters from Spain, was forced to reconsider his attitude toward the Jesuits, who had become increasingly disliked by autocrats in Italy, France and Spain. In 1773 they were suppressed by Pope Clement XIV.

The growth of democratic sentiment paved the way for the Napoleonic period, 1796 to 1814. Napoleon attempted to establish republics in Milan, Genoa, Naples and Rome. The latter lasted less than a year. The increasing disgust with the French finally caused the collapse of all these republics, and a reaction set in toward clerical and Austrian influence.

In 1798 Napoleon carried Pope Pius VI to France, only to have him die on his hands, and a new Pope was elected in Rome. The rule of Pius VII over the Papal States was conceded, and Napoleon arranged a Concordat between the Cisalpine Republic at Milan and the Holy See. In 1808 the struggle between Napoleon and Pius VII resulted in the annexation of the Papal States and the carrying off of Pius VII into captivity at Fontainebleau. This Pope did not die on his hands, but his capture was followed by the collapse of the Napoleonic rule in 1814. Pope Pius VII returned to Rome and was given back his territory.

From 1815 onward a general reaction in the Italian States towards revolution and the growth of liberalism led to the Risorgimento and the creation of modern Italy.

Signora Taigi described long before they occurred, the capture of Rome by the French in 1797, the captivity of Pius VII under Napoleon from 1809 to 1814, and even the fall of the temporal power in 1870. She foretold many purely secular events, such as the July Revolution of 1830. She made some mistakes, but these may have been due to misinterpretations of what she saw.

She predicted a great temporal triumph of the Church in terms that led her friends to believe that it would be realized under Pius IX ; but nothing of the sort occurred — unless we interpret the prediction as fulfilled in the Vatican settlement with the Fascist State.

MOTHER ELIZABETH SETON
[1774-1821]

MOTHER SETON was an American, and during her early years and in her married life she was an Episcopalian, a communicant of old Trinity Church at the head of Wall Street in New York. Her girlhood and young womanhood were radiant with happiness; but the shadow of suffering soon fell upon her. She did not rebel, but accepted it patiently as a divine indication that she was to take up the cross and follow her Saviour. She progressed from faith to faith; and through the persistent effort to conform her will with the will of God, she became a holy woman. Her cause has been introduced at Rome and a hundred thousand Americans are praying that she may be glorified.

I

WHAT stands out most vividly in her girlhood was the beautiful relationship with her father, Doctor Richard Bayley. He had married Catherine Charlton, the daughter of an Anglican clergyman, who died when Elizabeth was in her third year. Though Doctor Bayley married again and had other children, he showed marked devotion to Elizabeth and her younger sister Mary. The education of Elizabeth and the formation of her character appeared to be his supreme concern. He tried to inculcate in her the principles of right thinking and an amiable character, which he considered essential if she was to endear herself to others and become truly happy. From her earliest years he taught her to curb her natural vivaciousness out of regard for others. As Doctor Bayley's second wife had seven children of her own to look after, she was doubtless glad to leave these two girls to the special care of their father.

Elizabeth was entering her eleventh year when the war for American Independence came to an end. During the time of the British occupation of New York, Doctor Bayley, who was a Loyalist, served on the staff of Sir Guy Carleton in the capacity of surgeon. Elizabeth therefore grew up under conditions of privation and anxiety. The severe winter of 1780 brought dire suffering and reduced the city to a state of famine. She heard much of the cruelties inflicted upon American prisoners ; and of barbarities perpetrated up state by the Indians, who were the allies of the British.

From early childhood she learned to love God and was never happier than when she was engaged in prayer or spiritual reading. She relished especially the lives of the saints and became familiar with the Bible and the *Imitation of Christ*. She attended with fervor the services of Trinity Church at the foot of Wall Street and took naturally to practices of piety. She had a devotion to her Guardian Angel and reverently bowed her head when the Holy Name was pronounced. She examined her conscience each night and kept a list of her sins. She made frequent use of the prayer of Saint Augustine :

"My God, may I know Thee, and may I know myself !"

After the war the Bayleys did not undergo the same reverses of fortune as many of their loyalist friends. Doctor Bayley's character and professional reputation were such that his fellow citizens secured for him the high post of Inspector General in the New York Department of Health. In 1792, he was appointed to the Chair of Anatomy in the newly created Department of Medicine in Columbia College.

When Elizabeth Bayley, a charming girl of nineteen, was married in Trinity church to William Seton in January 1794, everything pointed to a prosperous and unruffled future for both of them.

He was a young man of English parentage who would soon inherit the chief share in a rich ship-owning firm. The Setons like the Bayleys were among the socially prominent families in New York.

These two young people were deeply in love, and their tastes and inclinations were harmonious. Five children were born to them within a few years: Anna Maria in 1795, William in 1796; and then came Richard, Catherine and Rebecca in rapid succession, the last being born in 1802.

The family was soon overwhelmed with calamities. In the war between England and France, the latter suspected America of partiality toward England; and French pirates seized many American ships. It became precarious to send a ship across the Atlantic, and the Seton firm was one of the first to feel the blow to their foreign trade. Its business melted away. At this juncture William Seton's father died, and though William was only thirty years of age, he had to look after his brothers and sisters as well as his own growing family. He might have shouldered this added burden, but soon his own health began to fail, and he developed symptoms of tuberculosis.

Shortly before the birth of their fifth child, Elizabeth's father, Doctor Bayley, who had been working night and day in the yellow fever epidemic, succumbed to the dreaded malady after an illness of only seven days. His favorite daughter nursed him constantly. After the third day he looked into her face and said : "The hand of God is in all this : nothing more can be done."

He suffered extreme pain and often cried out, "Christ Jesus, have mercy on me!" Finally, clinging to his daughter's hand, he breathed his last.

It was under the guidance of such a God-fearing father that Elizabeth Seton had acquired habits of Christian resignation. Throughout her life whatever befell her, she never lost faith in God. At that moment of overwhelming grief and dejection of spirit, she resorted to prayer and applied herself as usual to her daily tasks.

In consequence of his steady decline in health, William Seton was advised by his doctor to leave his business and spend the winter in sunny Italy. He had been there for several years before his marriage as a guest of the Filicchi brothers in Leghorn, with whom the Seton firm had business relations. He felt that the sea voyage would help him recruit his failing strength ; so he arranged to take his wife and their eldest child Anna Maria to spend several months with the Filicchi family.

They took passage on an American brig, *The Shepherdess*, which set sail on October 2, 1803.

After seven weeks the ship dropped anchor at the port of Leghorn just as the bells were ringing the Ave Maria. William Seton's health had improved during the voyage and he and his wife were buoyant with hope as they beheld the sunlit shores of Italy.

But it was not to be! Government officials boarded the vessel and ordered that, owing to the yellow fever epidemic in New York, all passengers from that port must be detained in quarantine for four weeks. The Seton family were led like prisoners to the Lazaretto where they were confined in a room with high arched ceilings, brick floor and stone walls, a mattress spread on the floor and no provision for heating.

Elizabeth Seton's diary, which she kept on her voyage and during the month of their incarceration in the Lazaretto, is an eloquent tribute to her character. She never complained, but took everything cheerfully as permitted by a loving God for their good. Though deprived of the consolations which their Church could have given them, yet Elizabeth's prayers and daily readings from the Bible and the Book of Common Prayer strengthened her courage and inspired her husband and daughter to submit humbly to God's will.

Elizabeth testified to her husband's spiritual progress:

"He very often says that this is the period of his life which, if he lives or dies, he will always consider as blessed, the only time which he has not lost. Not the smallest murmur, and the lifting of the eyes is the strongest expression I have yet heard from him in the rapid progress of his complaint which has reduced him almost to nothing."

William Seton died nine days after their release from quarantine, two days after Christmas. On Christmas day he had said to his wife:

"How I wish we could have the Sacrament!"

But there was no chaplain of the English Church in Leghorn, so that was impossible. His wife said however:

"Well, we must do what we can."

Accordingly she put a little wine in a glass and read suitable psalms and prayers which she had marked in her prayer-book, and they drank together the "cup of thanksgiving," ignoring the sorrows of time in view of the joys of eternity.

II

ELIZABETH SETON'S conversion to the Catholic Church was due primarily to God; but instrumentally to an Italian Catholic family, the Filicchis, and especially to Antonio Filicchi. Another disposing cause was her own refusal to settle down and remain satisfied with what she had.

The Filicchis took Elizabeth Seton and her daughter Anna to their home in Leghorn ; and throughout their stay in Italy showed them the most affectionate hospitality. Mrs. Seton had the privilege of visiting Florence in Signora Filicchi's company, and went with her frequently to the church of the Annunziata and the church of San Lorenzo.

One Sunday morning, she saw held up, for her adoration, a white Host in consecrated fingers. That moment marked a crisis in her life.

This visit in the Filicchi home opened Elizabeth Seton's eyes to the realities of Catholic family life — so different from the distorted notions of it which she heretofore entertained. Their piety and virtue, their devotion to one another, their love for the poor, necessarily directed her attention to their religion. If the practice of the Catholic faith could produce such interior holiness, she felt that she must learn more about their Church.

Her interest was quickened by the fact that Signora Filicchi kept strictly the fast of Lent, eating nothing until three o'clock each day. Writing to Rebecca, her sister-in-law, she said :

Well, Rebecca, they believe that all we do and suffer, if we offer it for our sins, serves to expiate them. You may remember when I asked Mr. Hobart what was meant by fasting in our prayer-book, as I found myself on Ash-Wednesday morning saying so foolishly to God : "I turn to you with fasting, weeping and mourning," and I had come to church after a good breakfast and full of life and spirits with little thought of my sins ; you may remember that he said something very vague about it being an old custom and all that.

She also liked the idea of going to Mass every morning. "Think what a consolation !" she wrote to Rebecca. "Ah, how often you and I used to sigh, when you pressed your arm on mine of a Sunday evening, and say, 'no more till next Sunday,' as we turned from the church door which closed on us. You know, too, how we were laughed at for running from one church to the other on Sacrament Sundays that we might receive as often as we could."

One day she questioned Antonio Filicchi regarding the difference between his Church and hers. He told her that there was but one true religion, without which it was impossible to please God !

"Oh," she exclaimed, "if there is but one true religion and if no one can please God without it, where will all those people go who live outside its pale ?"

"I do not know," he replied. "Their final destiny depends upon the degree of enlightenment they have received. I only know the fate of those who can obtain the true faith if they ask it from God and look for it."

"I understand," she said with a smile, "you warn me to pray and seek, and embrace your belief."

"Pray and seek, is all I ask of you. Your dear William was the first friend of my youth ; you are his successor in my affection. Your soul is dear to Antonio and will always be dear to him. May the good and all-powerful God enlighten your understanding and fortify your heart, that you may discover and follow the true way which leads to eternal happiness. That is what I desire for you. And while waiting, do not cease to pray ; do not cease to knock at the gate."

That conversation left an indelible impression in Elizabeth Seton's mind.

Before her arrival in New York she had made her decision. She would put herself under instruction and be received into the Catholic Church. She carried a letter of introduction from Filippo Filicchi to John Carroll, the Bishop of Baltimore ; and if she had presented it at once, all would have been simple.

Instead she took the advice of Antonio, who accompanied her and Anna on their voyage home. Acting on this advice she informed the Rector of

Trinity church, the Rev. John Henry Hobart, and also her relations, of the resolution she had taken of abandoning her communion.

From early childhood Elizabeth had been under the spell of Mr. Hobart. As soon as he received her letter he called upon her and brought all his personal magnetism and erudition into action to prevent her from making this cataclysmic change in her religion. Her family and friends likewise put every obstacle in her path. Mr. Hobart urged her to make a thorough study of the question before she came to a decision, giving her many books to read which were calculated to shake her faith in the Church of Rome. Finally he persuaded her to abandon entirely her researches after the truth.

She had landed in New York on June 3, 1804, and from then to the following Epiphany her soul was torn by perplexity and doubt. She fell into complete despair and desolation, and resolved to drop all study of the question and absent herself from all religious services of any sort. She determined to remain in this state of mental and moral indifference until she was set free by death.

On the feast of the Epiphany instead of going to church, as had been her custom, she sat in her room plunged in mournful introspection. She carelessly took up a volume of Bourdaloue's sermons and turned to the one for Epiphany. This sermon proved to be another turning-point in her life. It seemed as if God spoke directly to her soul. She was especially struck by these words :

"There are in the Church of God doctors and priests, just as there have always been ; they are men authorized to guide you and who are only too willing to listen to you. Ask them, as your fathers, and then they will tell you what you must do."

She closed the book and wrote down her resolution :

"Speak, Lord, for Thy servant heareth ! Thy hour has struck. From now on, no hesitation, no weakness, no procrastination ! Holy Church of God teach, direct, call to thyself thy child, docile and faithful for evermore."

Humanly speaking, it was the persistence of Antonio Filicchi that carried her through this time of desolation and led her finally to make her submission to the authority of the Catholic Church. It was fitting that he should be the one to stand with her when she pledged her allegiance to Catholicism in Saint Peter's Church, Barclay Street, on March 15, 1805. On the feast of the Annunciation she received Holy Communion.

Writing on that day to Signora Filicchi she said that the first thought she remembered after receiving her Lord was :

"Let God rise ! Let His enemies be scattered ! It seemed to me my King had come to take His throne, and instead of the humble, tender welcome I had expected to give Him, it was a triumph of joy and gladness that the Deliverer was come."

III

WHEN Elizabeth Seton returned to New York, she found that her husband's firm was bankrupt and that she would be entirely dependent on her relatives for support and for the sustenance and education of her children. If she had remained an Episcopalian, this would probably have been simple.

Upon her reception into the Catholic Church, her relatives turned from her as if she had been smitten with a loathsome disease. Her whole social set, aside from two women friends, ostracized her and her children. But two of her sisters-in-law — Harriet and Cecilia Seton — still very young, were bound to her by ties of strong affection which nothing could break. The sister-in-law with whom she had been most intimate — Rebecca Seton, had died just before Elizabeth had landed in America.

But for Antonio Filicchi and Father O'Brien, the Dominican Rector of Saint Peter's church, and Father Cheverus of Boston, she would have been utterly destitute and alone. The Filicchi brothers gave her the right to draw on their bank account in New York whenever she was in need.

However, she was not the kind of woman who would long be content to live on charity. She was endowed with an excellent mind and a sound constitution; consequently she thought of trying to make her living by teaching. She decided on joining a Mr. and Mrs. White who were opening a private school for girls in New York. This would have the additional advantage of enabling her to keep her daughters with her.

This school had barely been opened when a whispering campaign was started against it by her former friends and associates. It was insinuated that she would instil Catholic ideas into the impressionable minds of her young pupils. At the end of three months the school had lost all of its pupils and was forced to close its doors.

Elizabeth thereupon arranged with a Mr. Harris to be one of the teachers in his school, and to receive boarding pupils under her care in a separate house. This plan might have succeeded had not Elizabeth's youngest sister-in-law, Cecilia Seton, announced at that time that she would become a Catholic. Though only fifteen years of age, she was turned out of her home by her angry parents, and immediately sought refuge with Elizabeth.

This aroused another storm of abuse and persecution. Two of Elizabeth's former pastors — Richard Moore and John Henry Hobart — visited all the families that had entrusted their children to Mrs. Seton's care. They declared in authoritative tones that these children must be removed from her school immediately and that she must be utterly abandoned by all good Protestants. They insisted that she was not a fit person to be in charge of these children.

Perhaps Mr. Moore and Mr. Hobart, in their misguided zeal, were unconscious instruments in the hands of Providence to prevent Elizabeth Seton from settling down for the rest of her life as a school teacher. With the door thus closed in her face, she was compelled to look elsewhere for the field of labor to which God was calling her.

At first she thought of going to Montreal and there establishing a girls' school in a Catholic community. The Filicchi brothers had both advised it, as they had many business connections in that city. The Bishop of Baltimore, however, advised her not to do so as he thought that the rigors of the Canadian winter would be too severe for her young children.

At this juncture there came into her life a priest of extraordinary holiness — Father du Bourg, who was himself the instrument under God for leading her to take up the work which has made her famous. He was one of the French Sulpician priests who had been driven out of France by the Revolution ; and at that time was the President of the Sulpician College of Saint Mary in Baltimore.

In August 1807 he offered the Holy Sacrifice in Saint Peter's church, New York City. Elizabeth Seton in widow's dress presented herself to receive Holy Communion. Her face was bathed with tears and her rapt devotion impressed the priest. A few hours later she called at the house of Father Cibour, one of the priests attached to Saint Peter's, and asked for the privilege of meeting Father du Bourg.

He recognized her at once as the woman who had received Communion that morning ; and had heard of her conversion and holy life. She spoke of the difficulties she had been experiencing and of her desire to find some work which would enable her to support her children. At the same time she wished that it might be a religious work. She told him that she must take her children with her, because if she left them in New York, they would be deprived of their faith.

Father du Bourg had been contemplating the

establishment of a Catholic school for girls in Baltimore. There was, however, no religious community in that city which could take up the work of teaching. He felt that Mrs. Seton had been sent by God to take charge of this work. He proposed that she associate with her some other pious women who would live under the rules of some community already established. She agreed to lay the matter before the Bishop of Baltimore for his advice and to consult Father Cheverus and Father Matignon.

They advised her to accept Father du Bourg's offer. Father Cheverus urged her not to act impulsively, but to await a more decided manifestation of the will of God. Father Matignon wrote :

I ask of God that he may bless your views, and give you the grace to fulfil them for His greater glory. You are destined, I think, for some great good in the United States and here you should remain in preference to any other location. For the rest, God has His moments which we must not seek to anticipate, and a prudent delay only brings to maturity the good desires which He awakens within us.

Elizabeth Seton waited nearly a year, in extraordinary privation. Father du Bourg returned to New York in the spring of 1808 and Mrs. Seton conversed with him in the home of Mrs. Barry. Someone spoke of certain vacant lands or lots belonging to Saint Mary's College and owned by the Sulpicians.

"Some vacant lots," said Elizabeth by way of a pleasantry. "Suppose I go there and ask for them ?"

"Come to us, Mrs. Seton," said Father du Bourg. "We will help you to form a plan of life which will shelter your children from the dangers which threaten them here ; you will find in Baltimore more consolations of faith than you could find elsewhere. We desire to found a school for those children whose parents wish them trained to piety. Why delay ? Without buying or building, we can rent a house. Courage is not wanting on your part, and the experience of the first year will enlighten you and your friends on the measures to be adopted for the future."

As may be conjectured, Mrs. Seton offered no objection beyond her want of capacity.

To this Father du Bourg replied, "Fear nothing ; we need example more than talent."

Following this conversation Elizabeth Seton opened a school for girls next to the chapel of Saint Mary's Seminary in Baltimore. She and her associates lived as religious, adopting a costume like that worn by some nuns in Italy. Cecilia Conway of Philadelphia joined her. Mr. Cooper of Virginia, a recent convert to the Church, died leaving to the school ten thousand dollars for the education of poor children in the faith. With this they bought a farm near Emmitsburg.

Mrs. Seton's sisters-in-law, Cecilia and Harriet Seton, joined the Community. Elizabeth Seton took vows privately before Archbishop Carroll and her daughter Anna. The Community was now transferred to Emmitsburg to take charge of the school. They endured many hardships, but their fervor carried them through and also attracted many new aspirants. In December, 1809, Harriet Seton died; and in April, 1810, Cecilia. They were both buried in Emmitsburg.

In 1810 Bishop Flaget obtained in France the rule of the Sisters of Charity of Saint Vincent de Paul. Three of the Sisters were selected to train them in this rule, but were forbidden by Napoleon to leave the country. The rule was approved by Archbishop Carroll in January, 1812. Elizabeth Seton was elected Superior in spite of her protest that part of her time must be devoted to the care of her children.

Anna died during her novitiate in 1812, taking her final vows on her death-bed. Mother Seton and eighteen Sisters made their vows on the 19th July, 1813.

MOTHER ELIZABETH SETON

Rebecca died in 1816, Richard died in Italy shortly after his mother's death in 1821, William entered the Navy and died in 1868. Mother Catherine Seton, the youngest daughter of Mother Seton, became the first postulant of the New York Sisters of Mercy and later was assistant mother of the community. She died in 1891 at the advanced age of ninety-one. She prepared many condemned criminals for death before their execution.

IV

A CHARMING young mother surrounded by her children, living in prosperous circumstances, beloved by her father, worshipped by her husband, ministering to the poor, faithful in the performance of her religious duties as she understood them — who could have been more happy and settled in her life than Elizabeth Seton? Yet Almighty God had need of her in the extension and development of the Catholic Church in the United States.

One by one Almighty God took away the foundations on which her life was built; father, husband, fortune, wealthy relatives, influential friends, social prestige. Gradually He substituted for them another support, a faithful Catholic family in Italy. He took away the old religious foundation, to which

[243]

she had once been so devoted, and substituted the Rock of Peter. He gave her new spiritual guides, distinguished for their holiness and wisdom, and led her forth into a strange land. Like Abraham she journeyed forth by faith, not knowing whither she went.

By making use of this woman's life, stripped of all human resources and advantages, God performed miracles. Roughly speaking, there are today about ten thousand Sisters of Charity in the United States, Canada, China and the West Indies ; and countless hospitals, asylums, schools and colleges. All these foundations owe their inspiration to Mother Seton. The influence of her holy life and prayers is felt today in every corner of America and beyond the seas.

PRAYER TO OBTAIN THE GLORIFICATION OF MOTHER SETON

O GOD who has shown Thyself wonderful in Thy servant Elizabeth Seton, by the sincerity and constancy with which she sought Catholic truth ; by the heroic generosity with which she embraced it after she had found it ; by the strength of soul which she never lost throughout all the trials to which Thou wast pleased to subject her ; and, finally, by the solid and tender piety which flowed from her intimate knowledge of the Holy Scripture ; deign, we beseech Thee, to glorify here on earth this valiant woman, to give her numerous imitators, and through their example, and her intercession, to bring into the Catholic Church those souls, who deceived by the sophisms of heresy still remain outside its fold.

These favors we beg in the name of our Lord Jesus Christ Thy Son, who liveth and reigneth with Thee in the unity of the Holy Ghost one God, world without end. *Amen.*

JAMES CARDINAL GIBBONS

Baltimore, March 26, 1900

THE MARRIED LIFE OF
CORNELIA CONNELLY
[1809-1879]

WITHOUT prejudging the question as to whether or not Cornelia Connelly was a saint — for that question can be answered only by the infallible teaching authority of the Church — we may inquire into the character of her spiritual life during the years when she lived with her husband and see if we may discover any signs that she was then walking in the way of perfection.

The first thing that impresses us in the life of this gifted and attractive young woman is her persistent search for the Truth. She longed for union with Him who is the Way, the Truth and the Life, and she would not be content until she found Him. She left the religion of her childhood, the Lutheran faith, and became an Episcopalian in her nineteenth year because she believed that the Episcopal Church taught the revealed Truth of Christ more fully. It was this change that brought her into relationship with Pierce Connelly who was then an Episcopal clergyman in Philadelphia. Against the wish of her

aunt with whom she was living, she married him at
the age of twenty-three. Four years later he was
converted to Catholicism and his wife did not hesitate to follow him. She wrote in a letter :

"Whatever may be my prejudices and in spite of the
horror which I have always felt for the Catholic religion,
I am glad to be able to tell you that I am ready to follow
my dear husband in what he believes to be the path of
duty."

She said in another letter to one of her friends :

"You ask me why Pierce has become mixed up in religious controversy — surely to discover the Truth. And
since he professes to be a teacher of the Truth, he is bound
to cease teaching that of which he is doubtful."

Shortly after their being received into the Catholic Church, as they had abundant means to travel,
they decided to visit Rome. They took an apart-
ment in the Via della Croce but a short distance away
from the church of the Trinità dei Monti, which
was to mean so much in her later life. They were
received hospitably by the members of the English
and American colonies in Rome, as might be expected
of two young people of such social charm and brilliant attainments. Cornelia became a warm friend
of the Princess Sulmona who before her marriage
was Lady Gwendoline Talbot, the daughter of Lord

Shrewsbury. Many think that this young woman was a saint and there is talk of introducing her cause for beatification. Under the influence of a distinguished and holy Jesuit director, Father Rosaven, Cornelia took the first steps in her extraordinary spiritual career. She began to understand something of the kind of life to which God had called her. Practical woman as she was, almost scrupulous in her self-examination, she felt from the beginning the predominant influence of the Holy Spirit in her life ; she recognized His guidance and gave herself up to it. She was rigorously obedient to her directors, but her life was more mystical than ascetic.[1]

During the ravages of an epidemic of smallpox it was necessary for her to take her two children out of Rome and she went to Frascati. Her husband went with Lord Shrewsbury to England. The beauty of Frascati during the summer months reminded her of "a closed garden where God is pleased to dwell with the soul in secret and where He condescends to love and let Himself be loved with an intensity which surpasses all that human love could imagine."

A financial crisis in America brought about the loss of their fortune, and Pierce Connelly and his wife

---

[1] See the admirable *Life of Cornelia Connelly*, by a Religious of her Order, p. 17.

were compelled to return to make their living. He found work, teaching in a Catholic College near New Orleans at Grand Coteau ; Cornelia taught singing at the Convent of the Sacred Heart nearby. While there she made her first retreat. In later life she attributes to that retreat her real conversion and says that all subsequent retreats and other graces she received only emphasized and perfected the ideal and the outline sketched by the Holy Spirit at this time. She was fortunate in finding a skilful director, the Reverend Father Abadie, of the Society of Jesus. Later he said of her : "Ah, what a superb soul she had ! And first I was obliged to moderate her ardor and her spirit of sacrifice, and I prevented her from pushing too far penances and mortifications of every kind, for her obedience was astonishing, truly perfect ; and although a Catholic of hardly two years she had an intense interior life which was very sure and very true."

She loved her life as wife and mother and loved also the joys and the labors which she transformed and supernaturalized without ever surrendering them. We learn from her resolution in retreat that she reproached herself for her lack of order and resolved to make every month a day's retreat passing in review her duties as wife, as mother, as mistress of the household. She also resolved to live according to a rule "to live in the world a holy life and procure the spiritual and temporal well-being of my family: husband, children and servants."

It seems extraordinary that this young woman of twenty-nine, endowed with all sorts of personal gifts and favors, should so early have arrived at a stage in the spiritual life when she longed to give all to God and to suffer for His sake. Her director has testified that she lived in the practice of the third degree of humility, which Saint Ignatius has thus defined: "The state in which a soul looking upon Jesus Christ Our Lord, poor, humble and suffering, feels herself vanquished by love and rejection of love of self, throws herself upon Him and prays that she may suffer with and for her Well-Beloved, choosing freely poverty, humiliations and suffering in order to resemble Him more closely." It was in this attitude of soul that she faced one of the great crises of her life. On a beautiful day in January, 1840, she was sitting under the great trees not far from her little home where she could hear the laughs and cries of her children and she felt overcome with the sense of the beauty of creation and her own happiness. That is the moment when she offered this prayer: "My God, if all this happiness is not for Thee, for Thy glory and the good of my soul, take it from me, I surrender it to Thee."

We all know how but a little later her youngest son, scarcely more than a baby, had fallen into a cauldron of boiling sugar and after forty-three hours of terrible torture had died. God had begun to answer her prayer: He had taken this little one from the trials and uncertainties of this world and had deprived her of one of her choicest treasures. From that moment she had a profound devotion to Our Lady of Sorrows.

Very soon after this heart-breaking catastrophe, Pierce Connelly announced to his wife that he felt a vocation to be a priest and that she must make it possible for him by agreeing to take the vow of chastity and if possible enter the religious life. She who had been so supremely happy in her married life and in her home, was momentarily shocked at the idea of making so tremendous a sacrifice. The shadow of the Cross had indeed fallen across her life, but it was not long before she made the great surrender. She said to her husband: "However great may be the sacrifice, if God demands it of me I am ready to offer it to Him with all my heart and with all my soul." It is not difficult to imagine what a wrench this must have meant to Cornelia Connelly. She wrote in a letter to Monsignor McClosky, afterwards Cardinal Archbishop of New York:

"Is it really necessary that Pierce should make this sacrifice and that he should sacrifice me also ? I love my husband, I love my children with all my soul, is it necessary that I abandon them ?"

After a retreat of ten days she announced her consent to the separation, and her husband departed with Mercer, their son, to put him in college in England at Stonyhurst. Cornelia left her home and took up residence at the Convent with Adeline and little Frank. Her submission to the will of God in all this upheaval of her life was truly extraordinary. In these earlier years of the life of Cornelia Connelly we see exemplified what became the guiding principle of her whole life : perfect submission to the will of God. She took up the Cross daily and followed after Christ ; this is, He Himself has told us, the condition which He lays upon all his followers. As she expressed it in her own words :

"We glorify God by accomplishing His will as He makes it known to us through those who represent Him, and by the events in our lives which He orders or permits."

Another one of her sayings is to the same effect : "Take the Cross He sends, as it is, and not as you imagine it ought to be."

However much we may admire those who have inflicted upon themselves self-chosen penances of the most gruesome sort, we may be permitted to feel greater confidence in the method of Cornelia Connelly; in taking what God sends we may feel greater security and assurance than in choosing our own favorite form of mortification.

Mother Connelly began walking in the way of perfection when she lived in the Via della Croce in Rome: it was indeed to be the Way of the Cross. The root of the matter was in her then, all the events of the subsequent years of her life were but a flowering and bearing of fruit. Space and the purpose of this book do not permit us to go further into the trials and labors of Mother Connelly, nor into the story of her foundation of a great educational congregation — the Society of the Holy Child Jesus. The general trend of her life never changed: the same constant submission to the will of God, which made her life so abundantly fruitful in after years, was the animating motive of her life as a wife and a mother.

LOUIS VEUILLOT
[1813-1883]

I

Louis Veuillot sprang from the common people. His father was a cooper. He had no schooling after he was thirteen years old, but went to work in a lawyer's office. Later he drifted into journalism, serving in turn on several small country newspapers conducted in the interest of the bourgeois class. He made good use of his evenings by studying literature and history.

As he belonged by birth to the proletariat, he wondered at times if he were not a traitor to his class in working on such newspapers. He doubted too whether the materialistic culture of the Voltairian bourgeoisie was worth defending. As he had grown up with almost no religious education, his attitude toward the Church remained entirely negative. He knew nothing of Catholic principles, but bore no ill-will against the Church. As a youth he felt utterly uncertain about his future and had no idea that he could devote his talents to any high end.

His first intellectual shock came in 1831 from the conversion of a *confrère* in journalism, Gustave Olivier. He was astounded that so intelligent a man could become a Catholic. Later on Olivier invited him to go as his guest on a journey to Italy and the Orient. Veuillot, in describing the journey later, said he had thought of going to Constantinople, but he went further — he went to Rome!

In one of his earliest books — *Rome and Loreto* — he tells how Rome led him to the feet of Our Lady and how her prayers brought about his conversion. He was received into the Church in Rome and shortly afterwards made a retreat with the Jesuits at Fribourg. The retreat was an exhilarating experience to him and he found it difficult to leave this peaceful haven to return to the world. Nevertheless he became convinced that it was his vocation to devote his life to Catholic journalism and the defence of the Church ; and inspired by this new aim he sought work in France.

He first accepted a post under the Minister of the Interior. During his leisure hours he wrote several books in which he tried to set forth the attractiveness of the teaching and life of the Catholic Church. In 1839 he published his book, *Pilgrimages in Switzerland,* which was a brilliant success. In 1841 he followed it up with *Rome and Loreto* and a little later wrote a book on Algeria. Shortly afterwards he gave up his Government position, as he disliked administrative work. He admitted that he "never could support any other chain than that of Christian morality and the Divine will."

He soon discovered in the *Univers* the journal through which he might carry out his mission as the bold and ardent champion of ultra-montane Catholicism. It had been founded in 1833, but was comparatively unknown and without financial backing. Veuillot refused a flattering offer in political life and became editor of this paper in 1843. In a surprisingly short time his daring, talent and wit had transformed it into the leading organ of Catholic thought in Europe.

He was bitterly opposed by the secularist press as well as by liberal Catholics, but he gained ever-increasing renown by his ably written and uncompromising editorials. During the Vatican Council in 1870 he was one of the most effective defenders of papal infallibility. He is now commonly regarded, even by free-thinkers, as one of the most readable French writers of the nineteenth century.

He accepted no honors, not even election to the French Academy or decorations from the Pope. His one desire was to serve. He had humbly consecrated his life to the defence of Catholic truth and he never deviated from that course.

From 1860 to 1867, the *Univers* was suppressed by the Government for publishing the Encyclical of Pius IX, *Nullis Certe,* which criticized the Napoleonic policy. During these seven years he carried on his journalistic mission through books and pamphlets.

Veuillot insisted that he belonged to no party. He had only two loyalties: one was to the Church and the other to his country. The Church, he said, tolerated all forms of government, provided only that those who held the power used it for the good of the people and according to the laws of God. The government, he contended, must respect the rights of God and the Church. In thus pleading for the freedom of the Church from State oppression and control, he became consistently the apostle of liberty. "Liberty through the truth" was his aim. It was the true liberty he was seeking, not the empty sentiment inscribed on walls or written in copybooks. The spirit of the Revolution, in his opinion, was necessarily destructive of all true liberty.

The French positivist writer, M. Jules Lemaître, said of him: "This Catholic has spent his life in fighting despotism and hypocrisies; and no one has more frequently or more boldly spoken in the name of liberty than this 'Jesuit,' this 'sacristan,' this 'partisan of the tyranny of the Church.'"

This intransigeant warrior was most tender and gentle as a son, a brother, a father, and the most faithful of friends. His private life is revealed chiefly through his letters, some of the most sparkling and witty being written to his friend, Mademoiselle Grammont — his senior by many years — who loved Veuillot "because he was not a dull somnambulist who talked in his sleep of an impossible dream of reconciling falsehood and truth, of amalgamating the Catholic Church with the Satanic Revolution."

His married life was compressed into seven years of unalloyed happiness. At the age of thirty-two he married Mathilde Murcier. In one of his letters he said that she was "not rich nor uncomely, not stupid, nor ill-bred — nothing out of the ordinary. She had a mind, but I knew nothing of it ; one would never have suspected its existence. It was, however, evident that she possessed habits of piety and an exquisite modesty."

He later made this brief confession : "I am happy and I am in love. To be happy and to be in love is the same thing ; provided that you understand it. Today I understand."

"My happiness," he wrote later, "would be complete if I did not find myself too happy, and experience the horrible fear of paying later for all these joys which I have not deserved." His presentment was unerring: his beloved wife was taken from him suddenly in 1852, leaving him with five small daughters.

He was overwhelmed with grief. When writing later of a visit to Chamonix where he and his wife had gone together on their wedding-trip, he said: "No, my God, my good and just Master, I would not weep; and if I wept, my tears would not accuse Thee! . . . She, whom Thou hast given me for a time has passed like time. What matters it that these flowers have withered, this music has ceased, this darkness has succeeded to the brilliant sunshine? What Thou hast given me for eternity I still possess, though I see her no more."

Seven years later he was writing to his sister-in-law. As he traced the address, Madame Veuillot, Rue du Bac 44, his hand trembled and the tears came. He remembered . . . "At present," he said, evoking the image of his lamented wife, "I praise God for having given her the better part, but never on this earth shall I offer this praise without my heart bursting with grief."

During the summer following his wife's death, three of his little girls died within three months!

The two remaining motherless children were brought up by Veuillot's sister, Elisa. In 1874 one daughter married Commander Pierron and the other, Lucie, became a nun.[1]

At that moment Veuillot sacrificed "the last flowers of his crown." His devoted sister Elisa had died some years before.

After his sister's death he wrote this tribute to her character : "I sketch here your noble and sweet countenance, embellished for us as for the angels by the cares which have worn you out before your time. You, who through love of God refused to give yourself to the service of God and through charity severed yourself from the joys of charity, you have not fully enjoyed either the peace of the cloister or the care of the poor or the apostolate in the world ; and your great heart has known how to deprive itself of all which was great and perfect like itself. You have shut up your life with little duties : the servant of a brother, the mother of orphans.

---

[1] The following obituary note appeared in the *Universe* (London), Sept. 1, 1933 :

Mère Marie des Anges who died last week at the Abbaye aux Bois, Paris, was the daughter of the eminent Louis Veuillot. She became a nun of Canonesses Regular of St. Augustine and showed all the remarkable learning of her father.

When the convents were closed in Paris by the French Government, she helped with some of the other nuns to open a school, and during the last years, when the Abbaye became a club and college for students, she took an active part in its organisation. All her life she endured great suffering and died a holy death at the age of 73, in the 47th year of her religious profession.

There you remained like the most attentive spouse
and the most patient mother — giving yourself completely and receiving only half as much. You have
sacrificed youth, liberty, your future. You were no
longer yourself, you became one who existed no
more : the departed wife and the mother who was
buried. You offered your days and nights to those
who did not call you their mother, and you have
shed the tears of a mother upon the graves which
were not those of your children. And in this ab-
negation and these sorrows you sought and found
for the help of others still more infirmities to suc-
cor, still more feeble ones to sustain, still more
wounds to cure. May you be blessed of God as you
are in our hearts !"[1]

II

THIS versatile French journalist and man of letters
was essentially a fighter. He made violent attacks
on the University of Paris, the Second Empire and
the leaders of United Italy for their conquest of the
Papal State. Above all he was in frequent combat
with liberal Catholics. He was a fiery champion of
Catholicism in its most ultramontane form. No
doubt the liberals of his day thought of him as an
intolerable bigot ; yet he exerted a salutary and brac-

[1] *Louis Veuillot,* by C. Lecigne, p. 137.

ing influence on Catholicism in nineteenth century France, and was probably instrumental in making it the vital force which it is today.

While liberal Catholics were concerned chiefly with commending the faith to men of science and the anti-clerical world generally, Louis Veuillot had quite other objectives in view. To the criticism that his miliant tactics would never convert souls he replied :

"That is not what I am aiming at ; I am striving rather to wake up, to stimulate, to convert the faithful ; to inspire them to march to battle and get them into it somehow in spite of themselves. Whenever I see one of them waking up out of his torpor,—if I have been in the slightest degree responsible—I congratulate myself on my success. For I have turned a lifeless statue into a man, I have opened a mouth that was shut, I have rendered fit for fighting an arm that was listless. If I can thus arouse Catholics to their duty, they will convert the wicked!"[1]

No doubt he sometimes exaggerated because of the sincere repulsion he felt for the method of "sweetness and light." He might have been more just in his encounters with Frederick Ozanam. Saint Paul said there were "diversities of graces, but the same Spirit." Veuillot would have found it

[1] C. Lecigne's *Life*, p. 163.

difficult to appreciate that sentiment. He could not forget that he had seen "France spit on the Church !" To this insult he felt that only one answer was possible ; and he delivered that answer like a blow from the shoulder. It was probably true that many liberal Catholics had long been too indulgent.

There is no reason why we may not at the same time approve of the warlike courage of Veuillot and the miracles of charity of Ozanam ; of the wisdom of the serpent and the harmlessness of the dove. In the tactics of Catholic propaganda more than one method is legitimate. Veuillot felt that it was his vocation to be a watchman and a soldier. When Ozanam accused him of discouraging conversions, he replied :

We wish indeed that the blasphemers might be saved, but we are not willing that in the meantime they should destroy the souls of other men. If we cannot rescue our brethren from them without inspiring them with an eternal hatred against the Christian name, we do well to be on bad terms with them. It is important no doubt that they should be saved, but it is also important that they cease to destroy us. No one could say that each of their souls is worth two of ours, still less a hundred or a thousand. Besides we would like to know from the point of view of eternity what harm we are doing them in preventing them from increasing the amount of evil in the world. We count their victims by the hundred and in our own souls the remains of their poisons still linger ! It is our business to escape today from their diabolical wiles.

It ought to have been easy for two such saintly men as Veuillot and Ozanam to understand each other. Was it necessary for Ozanam to begin homilies on charity by attacks on the avenger of the Church or to accuse Veuillot of "presenting the truth to men not by the side which attracts them, but by that which repels them," and of "exciting the passions of the faithful"? Ozanam perhaps was not the best authority on the duties of the Catholic soldier, for he was pre-eminently a peacemaker. Veuillot likewise was not sufficiently alive to the need of an unique strategy in the defence of religion against the newer forms of unbelief.

III

VEUILLOT had a private audience with the Holy Father Pius IX on the twenty-third of February, 1859. The Pope said to him : "You have always been on the right track ; and you will not depart from it." This was high commendation of the methods and the principles which Veuillot had followed throughout his journalistic career. What then were these principles, which thus obtained the seal of papal approval?

Before the French Revolution, a régime of Christian social order had prevailed for many centuries under the Catholic monarchy of France. The State was distinct from the Church, but not separated from it. They lived together like a husband and wife, under the same roof, in perfect harmony of thought and affection. They quarrelled now and then, but in the main a cordial and intimate concordat was maintained between the Church and the State; and they were bound together in the common defence of Christian truth, social peace and national greatness.

One of the fixed aims of the French Revolution was to effect a divorce between the Church and the State. The leaders of the Revolution attributed no importance to the revealed teachings of the Catholic Church. Like Pilate, they asked, "What is truth?" To them religious truth was nothing but opinion and they held that each man could believe as he liked. Thus they rejected the teaching authority of the Church; they abolished in fact all authority, control, censure. Theoretically they allowed free speech and a complete freedom of the press. Their goal was to laicize and secularize all spiritual institutions. They taught that the will of the people was sovereign and introduced the modern code which holds that the State is atheist and ought to be so.

Henceforth not only in France but elsewhere in Europe two powers were in conflict: Revelation

and the Revolution. Each denied the other ; each
was necessarily the contradiction of the other.

What was the Catholic Church to do in face of
the anti-Christian falsehood proclaimed in 1789?
It was impossible for her to admit that error had
the same rights as the truth, that disorder is a good
thing, or that chaos is a harmony. Consequently
through her Supreme Pontiffs she rejected the root
principles of the new social order. Pius VI in 1791,
Pius VII in 1814, Gregory XIII in 1832, Pius IX
in 1864 — all condemned the fundamental tenets
of the French Revolution.

Yet the Catholic Church must live even in the
midst of revolutionary chaos. Consequently she
adapted herself as best she could to the circumstances.
For the sake of the general peace she sacrificed, not
her principles, but the right of vindicating them.
The Church did not support all that was connoted
by 1789 ; on the contrary she denied and repudi-
ated it. She resigned herself to it only as to a
brutal fact which she hoped would be only temporary. She asked her children to take the same
view of the Revolution as she did ; and instead of
consecrating it by an entire acceptance she demanded
that they work with all their energy for the restoration of the Christian social order that had prevailed

when the Church and the State were in harmony with each other.

At this point Catholic Liberalism intervened. It proposed the monstrous marriage of the Revolution and Revelation. Veuillot saw at once the seductive power which this proposal might exercise on the Church. It reminded him of the story of the Temptation in the Gospel.

The Church is poor and hungry : let her be liberal and she will be rich ; the stones will be changed into bread ! But the hunger which torments the Church, as it did Jesus, is charity. The Church is longing to nourish perishing souls. The bread which she wishes to distribute, which alone can make them strong, is the word which proceeds from the mouth of God — the Truth. Liberalism says to her, "if you are of God, if you have the word of God, you risk nothing in leaving the pinnacle of the Temple : cast yourself down ; go to the multitude which no longer comes to you, divest yourself of all that displeases them, tell them the things that they like to hear, and you will reconquer them, for God is with you !" But the words which the crowd loves to hear are not the words that proceed from the mouth of God and it is always forbidden to tempt the Lord. Finally Liberalism pronounces its last word : "I hold power over the world and I will give you the world." But it makes always the same condition : *si cadens adoraveris me*. "Prostrate yourself on a level with those who have no God, and follow the people of substance whom I shall assign as your leaders, after they shall have sworn never to cross the threshold of a place of prayer :

then you will see how the world will honor you and listen to you, and how Jerusalem will be re-born more beautiful than ever !" [1]

M. de Falloux, Mons. Dupanloup, M. Montalembert and l'Abbé Lamennais had adopted the liberal creed of 1789. Opposed to them were such men as de Maistre, de Bonald, Donoso-Cortès and Veuillot. On the side of the latter were also the Pope and the Church. They saw clearly that the Revolution in its essence and aims was anti-Catholic; it wished above all things to overturn and destroy the Catholic Church.

As we view today the work of the legitimate heirs of the French Revolution, as they are operating in Russia, Spain and Mexico, can we doubt that Veuillot was right when he insisted that it was impossible to baptize the monster, to christianize 1789? "A vain dream," he exclaimed, "because the Revolution has raised up in the world and in all countries of the world a race deplorably ignorant whose perverse brain does not want liberty, because it does not want religion."

[1] C. Lecigne, *op. cit.*, pp. 174 *et seq.*

FREDERIC OZANAM
[1813-1853]

I

FREDERIC OZANAM was born in Lyons of devout Catholic parents. His religion was essentially home-made. For the first seventeen years of his life, he saw the Catholic religion practised daily by his parents, and they trained him in habits of prayer and worship. He also had the advantage of a wise spiritual director, the Abbé Noirot. His father, a physician, gave freely of his services to the poor. He impressed upon Frederic the necessity of fitting himself to earn his own living, and to support the family if need arose.

His first youthful enthusiasm was for philosophy. The Abbé Noirot told him that literature, religion and morality had produced great men, but that "they had been great only because they had drawn their knowledge from philosophy." The Abbé taught him to link together his religion and his philosophy in the service of humanity. Henceforth the defence of the faith became his chief intellectual concern. In his ardent eclecticism as a philosopher he was confident that he could make Descartes, and even Kant, defenders of the faith !

He soon realized that to prepare himself adequately for this apologetic task he must know something of the comparative history of religions. This study he carried on in his leisure moments ; for in his eighteenth year, in obedience to his father's wishes, he went to Paris to study law.

To the onlooker he was simply one more student in the throng of young men in the university centre ; but his subtle Lyonnais soul soon began to make itself felt on Mont Sainte Geneviève. In Ozanam there were qualities which do not usually go together. He was both mystical and practical ; mystical without being individualistic, practical without being worldly. Perhaps his most ingratiating quality was his humility : he had no pride of intellect.

Soon after arriving in Paris, Ozanam was invited to make his home with the famous scientist, Ampère. There he made the acquaintance of Ballanche, upon whom had fallen the mantle of Chateaubriand as the chief French apologist of Christianity. These two men convinced Ozanam of the value of the historical method in defending the Christian religion — a method which he later developed in his own fashion in his writings and lectures at the Sorbonne. Only, instead of defending Christianity as did Chateaubriand, he defended the Catholic Church.

At about this time Chateaubriand gave Ozanam a piece of advice, which indicates the sharp line of cleavage between the Church and the world in the Paris of that time. Before he left home, Ozanam's mother had made him promise that he would never attend the theatre. Chateaubriand reinforced this counsel by telling him : "You would gain nothing at the theatre, and might lose much." At any rate he did not swell the number of Lyonnais youths who took part in the tumultuous quarrels which followed the romantic dramas produced at the Comédie Française, nor did he join in their songs of praise to the glory of Victor Hugo.

It was not long before his faith was put to a severe test. He felt saddened and crushed by the terrible pressure of unbelief which surrounded him. Although he had set out to be an apologist for the Church, he became quite certain that he was unequal to the task.

At the age of nineteen he wrote to a friend : "I dislike Paris ; it is a lifeless city, with no faith, no love. It is like a vast corpse to which I am tied with all my youth and life ; its cold freezes me, its corruption kills me."

The faith of Ampère created about Ozanam an atmosphere unfavorable to doubt. As a young man, Ampère too had left Lyons for Paris. He had come to the capital with the firm resolve "never to lose sight of the light eternal"; and he too had to wrestle with the temptation of unbelief. When young Ozanam saw this learned scientist kneeling at Saint Étienne du Mont, "beside the poor widow and the little child, less humble than he"; when one evening in the scientist's study, he heard the old man — holding his large head in his hands — exclaim, "How great is God, Ozanam, how great is God!" and when Ampère said to him one evening during the cholera epidemic, "If this night I feel myself taken ill, Ozanam, I will rap on the wall with my cane. Run and seek my confessor!" — he felt something give way in his soul before the invigorating thrust of this old man's faith.

Ozanam himself has told us that it was his old confessor, the Abbé Noirot, who finally brought him safely through this crisis in his life. He wrote: "I knew all the horror of doubts that torment the soul. It was then that the instructions of a priest and philosopher (Abbé Noirot) saved me. I believed thenceforth with an assured faith, and touched by so rare a goodness, I promised God to devote my life to the services of the truth which had given me peace."

By temperament and training Ozanam was a man of democratic sympathies, and was naturally attracted to the brilliant triumvirate who were the editors of *L'Avenir* · Lamennais, Lacordaire and Montalembert. They chose as their motto, "God and Liberty," and aimed at cementing the bonds between the Church and the working classes, and at securing political liberty and equal rights for all people. They soon came into sharp conflict with the new Republican religion of Saint-Simonism, or Socialism ; to counteract it they aimed at the catholicising of liberalism. Owing to papal disapproval, they discontinued the publication of *L'Avenir* in 1833. The triumvirate finally fell apart, and their efforts to amalgamate Catholicism with what they conceived to be political freedom came to an end. Lamennais gave up Catholicism and threw himself wholly into the fight for liberty. Lacordaire clung to Catholicism and withdrew from the political arena altogether. Montalembert, more free to act perhaps because he was a layman, refused to surrender either the Catholic faith or his democratic ideals.

The papal condemnation of Lamennais did not greatly disturb Ozanam and his friends. They had been more strongly drawn to the Abbé Lacordaire from the first, and found in him an intelligent defender of the faith whom they could follow unreservedly.

After the defection of Lamennais, Ozanam wrote : "We were putting our trust in the words of a man ; and God put his hand on the mouth of this man, in order that we might learn how to be Christians without him, and to teach us that we must detach ourselves from everything, except the faith and virtue."

II

ONE day young Ozanam, after hearing a lecture by Silvio Pellico, the Italian authority on prison-life, wrote down this reflection : "Christianity is for me a sphere of ideas and of worship ; but not sufficiently a sphere of morality, of intention, of action."

It was this resolution that saved him from a life of barren intellectualism, of faith without works ; and gave him the first impulse to found the Society of Saint Vincent de Paul. Throughout the rest of his life, his works of active charity were a protection against discouragement in the dark hours when he could see only "pride among the intellectuals, fatuity among the worldly, and debauchery among the common people." The defence of the faith and the love of the poor became the two master passions of his life.

From 1830 to 1850, Europe was in a ferment of political upheaval and social unrest, which culminated in the revolutions of 1848. Thrones were tottering, democratic ideas were spreading everywhere. Mazzini was carrying on his bizarre propaganda for a world-wide Catholicism without priests or Pope — a secularized universal brotherhood. In many minds the Catholic Church was identified with the policies of reaction and obscurantism. In France, the prevailing tendency was sceptical and anticlerical. In the University of Paris, practically all the professors were hostile to the Church and prophesied the speedy demise of Christianity.

Ozanam and his friends among the students warmly sympathized with the new democratic movement, but in their case the spirit of revolt — so congenial to youth — manifested itself in another direction than a challenge to kings and emperors. Ozanam challenged the dictatorial pronouncements of those other sovereigns, the university professors who delighted in scoffing at the Catholic religion. He had the honor of obtaining from Letronne a retraction of an erroneous statement he had made about the Church. When Jouffroy accused the Church of repudiating science and liberty, Ozanam secured fifteen signatures among his students to a vigorous protest, in response to which the professor of philosophy apologized for wounding the religious susceptibilities of his hearers.

In 1832, with the help of Bailly, Ozanam inaugurated a conference on history, in which young men of all shades of opinion might debate historical questions. He wrote to a friend concerning this conference : "It is most necessary to make it clear to the student body that one can be a Catholic and have common sense, and that one can love both religion and liberty. We must try to pull these young men out of their religious indifference, and accustom them to grave and serious discussions." Above all he refused to be silenced by false historical assertions about religion and the Catholic Church.

In June, 1833, one hundred students, and in December two hundred more, signed with Ozanam two petitions to the Archbishop of Paris, for the provision of a series of sermons, new in their form, adapted to the controversies of the day, designed to show the applicability of Christianity to the needs of the individual and society, and to set forth a philosophy of the sciences, the arts, and human life. In response to this request the Archbishop asked seven priests to preach successively at Notre Dame during Lent on some such subjects ; but the success of the course was not reassuring. The next Lent, Lacordaire gave the first of his famous conferences, and five thousand men listened breathlessly. At their close, Ozanam said, "The world knows now that Christianity is alive."

These Lenten Conferences in Notre Dame have now been going on for a hundred years, and their influence has been incalculable. Today all Paris and a large part of France listen to them over the radio. They had their inception in the mind of Ozanam, when he was a university student of twenty.

In the month of May in the same year, he founded the first conference of the Society of Saint Vincent de Paul, for relief work among the poor. In this centenary year of the Society's existence, there are more than 11,000 conferences with over 200,000 active members.

The enemies of the faith supplied the spur that prodded Ozanam into action. His sceptical comrades at the Sorbonne said to him one day :

"If you speak of the past, you are right : Christianity has in former times worked marvels. But today Christianity is dead. In short, what are *you* doing, you who boast of being Catholics ? Where are the works that demonstrate your faith ?"

He founded the Saint Vincent de Paul Society not simply to be a work of Christian charity. Its first object, according to its primary rule, was to be the sanctification of its members. Ozanam held that faith could be maintained only by the practice of charity. He also intended his society to be a practical exemplification of the principles of true democracy; for he believed that the rights of man should be founded not on justice but on charity. The first social problem was the problem of poverty. If Catholic men were to fulfil their obligations towards their poorer neighbors, they could do so only by becoming their servants. Like their Master Christ they must become the servants of all. In ordinary philanthropy, men gave of their substance for the relief of the poor, but they did not give of their hearts.

Ozanam insisted that it was the sacred duty of every man to give; and that he who received help was giving quite as much as the one who helped him. He summed up his teaching in a new definition: "Almsgiving is a reward for service done which has no salary." It is a part payment of the debt we owe the poor. "They suffer where we do not; they serve God by suffering in a way that we do not: they win for us graces from Him, which without them we would never have; they make humanity itself more like Jesus." What could repay, he asked, the tears of gratitude in a mother whom we have helped, or the clasp of a laborer's hand when we have given him the chance to start again?

He refused to admit that the giving of an alms could ever be regarded as an act of condescension, or a mere bestowal of a favor. His indignation flared up whenever people spoke of almsgiving as a crime. Such people, he argued, would deprive the poor man of giving what he too had to give, "a word or an act of gratitude, the last of his possessions, but the greatest of all, for they are possessions which cannot be bought."

The Saint Vincent de Paul Society has never been content with the giving of alms; its members have always aimed at personal contact and a large-hearted service of those to whom they have ministered. The spirit which for a hundred years has animated these Catholic men of action shines forth in the ideals of the founder of the Society.

Almsgiving, Ozanam maintained, may be an honor, "when it takes hold of a man and lifts him up; when it looks first and foremost to his soul; when it attends to his training, religious, moral, political; when it helps him to freedom from his passions and his other bonds; when it leads him to real independence and makes him a truer man. Help is an honor and not a humiliation when to the gift of bread is joined a visit that comforts, a word of advice that clears away a cloud, a shake of the hand that revives a dying courage ; when it treats the poor man with respect, not only as an equal, but in many ways as one above us, since he is with us as one sent by God himself, to test our justice and our charity, and by our own attitude towards him to enable us to save our souls."

The work of the Society had a two-fold effect on Ozanam and the students who were banded together with him in these tasks. Primarily it convinced them of the truth of their religion. Troubled — as many young men are — by doubt, and surrounded by those who had become sceptical or indifferent or had taken up with the new religion of Saint-Simonism, these young men found their faith reviving under the bracing exercise of charity.

It also convinced them practically of the sins of the social order under which they were living, and the urgent need of reform. While visiting the homes of the very poor, they could not but condemn a civilization which not only generated but tolerated such social misery. Ozanam saw "a new feudalism of irresponsible wealth trying to plant its ignoble tents on the sepulchres of the Middle Ages." He was convinced that he and his companions were called to be "defenders, moderators and guides, of the interests of the masses."

[280]

To this end he instituted courses of lectures and study circles for working men, and soon founded a journal to propagate his ideas, which he called *L'Ère Nouvelle* — dubbed by his opponents, "The New Error."

The first lesson which Ozanam was to draw from the Revolution of 1848 was the duty of Catholics to re-establish points of contact with the oppressed laboring classes, and to study the objects for which they were fighting: organization of the workers, leisure for recreation, and a living wage. This sort of study would have been more useful before the revolution than after it; but Ozanam could not be held responsible for the slowness of French Catholics to realize their social duties, and we must remember that he was writing forty years before the Encyclical *Rerum Novarum* of Pope Leo XIII.

III

In May 1835 Ozanam won his licentiate in letters; and in July his doctorate in law. In spite of his scholastic successes, he fell into the depths of despondency. It may have been due to overwork. He spoke of his soul as "sterile sand which the rains of heaven water without making it fruitful." Returning to Lyons for his vacation, he confessed himself to be a "rock of egotism and pusillanimity, bargaining with God and with himself, counting by sous and pennies, abounding in words but poor in works."

In 1837 his father died from a fall on a dark staircase while visiting a poor patient, and Frederic knew he would have to take his father's place as head of the family. This made his future seem more obscure than ever, as he had little relish for the practice of law.

Overwhelmed with sadness, he poured out his soul to a priest in Lyons, who surprised him by replying, "Rejoice in the Lord always!"

Ozanam was comforted and afterwards said of this advice, "It required all the audacity, all the pious insolence of Christianity, to speak in that way. And yet Christianity is right!"

Two positions were open to him. A new chair in commercial law had been established in Lyons and Ozanam was invited to accept it. The other opening was in Paris. He had made a favorable impression at the Sorbonne with his thesis on the philosophy of Dante, on which he had worked for many months. Fauriel, who held the chair in comparative literature, was about to retire on account of age; and although not friendly to the Church, he suggested to Ozanam that he take the chair provisionally for a year, with the possibility of being elected as his successor.

The choice he had to make was further complicated by the inner struggle that was then occupying him concerning his vocation. Lacordaire had hoped that he might become a Dominican. The more Ozanam meditated on the lay activities to which he had committed himself, the more he became convinced that it was his vocation "to give some impetus toward happiness to the depressed French people, and through France to the entire world." In the course of 1840, his decision was taken: he would not join a Dominican Order of preachers.

Before the year ended he was engaged to be married. The Abbé Noirot, who had been the chief formative influence in his youth, now helped to settle his future destiny. Thanks to this priest, Frederic Ozanam and Amélie Soulacroix, the daughter of the Rector of the University of Lyons, pledged themselves to each other.

Ozanam left it to her to make the choice between Lyons and Paris. She, knowing well what it would mean to leave her home and her many friends in Lyons, and that the venture in Paris would be experimental, nevertheless decided that Paris offered the best sphere of usefulness for Ozanam's talents and that it was her duty to follow him there and assist him in his new life. In Paris he could continue as professor the rôle he had assumed as student ; he could devote himself to the defence of the faith, the service of youth and the visiting of the poor as long as God might spare him.

For Amélie Soulacroix, Frederic was a man of good will consecrated to God, upon whom God and the poor had already established claims which came before hers. She took this consecrated will for better or for worse, with its untold spiritual possibilities.

Lacordaire, far away in Paris, did not understand. Speaking to a friend of Ozanam's marriage, he called it a "snare." It was an unjust accusation, and M. Hello does not hesitate to condemn it.

It was typical of the character of Ozanam that he idealized what he loved. He cherished in his wife the feminine ideal which the women of classical Christian literature had inspired. She was the woman of whom Prudentius sang, for whom "everything became pure which she deigned to look upon with her eyes or touch with her foot" ; she was like Dante's Beatrice, the source of truth and virtue. He thought of her as more heavenly than earthly ; not as the daughter of Eve, but as the child of Mary.

Ozanam's exalted conception of marriage is

brought out in a passage from one of his later works, *The History of Civilization in the Fifth Century* :[1]

Marriage is something greater than a contract for it involves also a sacrifice. The woman sacrifices an irreparable gift, which was the gift of God and was the object of her mother's anxious care : her fresh young beauty, frequently her health, and that faculty of loving which women have but once. The man in his turn sacrifices the liberty of his youth, those incomparable years which never return, the power of devoting himself to her whom he loves, which is vigorous only in his early years, and the ambition — inspired by love — to create a happy and glorious future. All this is possible but once in a man's life, between the ages of twenty and thirty — a little earlier or a little later, perhaps never. Therefore Christian marriage is a double oblation, offered in two chalices : one filled with virtue, purity and innocence ; the other with unblemished self-devotion, the immortal consecration of a man to her who is weaker than himself, who was unknown to him yesterday, and with whom today he is content to spend the remainder of his life. These two cups must both be full to the brim, in order that the union may be holy, and that heaven may bless it.

During the brief span of his life, Ozanam's most important work in the eyes of his contemporaries was his professorship at the Sorbonne. Within a year after his marriage he was elected to succeed Fauriel in the chair of comparative literature. His lectures and writings did much to make the Church more respected in the intellectual world of his day.

[1] Vol. II, p. 66.

Although his oratorical gifts were not of a high order, he possessed unusual personal magnetism. His voice was inflexible, heavy and monotonous; his gestures lacking in grace; and his nervous fatigue evident to all. Yet his hearers knew that they were in the presence of a man, who—as Lacordaire put it—was compelled to unburden his soul to his audience and to convey his ideas with all the warmth and force which one must expend in the service of the truth. Renan attended his lectures as a young man, and said of him: "I never went out from his lectures without having been made stronger, and more determined to do great things . . . Ozanam, how we loved him!"

Ozanam wrote shortly before his own death, "Next to the infinite consolations which a Catholic finds at the altar, and next to the joys of family life, I have found no greater happiness than in speaking to young people of intelligence and heart." We may imagine the joy it brought him one day when a student said to him, "What numerous sermons have never succeeded in doing, you have done in one hour—you have made me a Christian!"

His method of apologetic was primarily historical. He showed what the Church had done for mankind in the past, and argued from that to what it could and should do in the present. He applied this argument with special cogency to the task confronting the Church in the revolutionary era culminating in 1848. Fourteen centuries earlier the Church had assisted, and in a sense presided, at the historical cataclysm which transferred the power and authority of the Roman Empire to the barbarians from the north. In 1848, such a transfer was apparently to be repeated, not from one race to another, but from one class to another.

If the Church was not annhilated, Ozanam argued, in the fifth century, why should it be disconcerted — much less annihilated — by the revolutionary novelties of the nineteenth? The thought which civilized the barbarians might still mould the chaos of Europe. This could be only if the Catholic faith were presented to the consciences of men one by one. It could not be accomplished suddenly by imperial decree, as it was by Constantine. To work for the re-establishment of Christianity by political means seemed to Ozanam to manifest a lack of faith.

He maintained to the end an invincible belief in Providence: in the divine guidance of the destinies of society and the Church, but also of the individual. He said once, in an address to workingmen, that we work out our destinies here below, but without knowing what function they will fulfil in the purposes of God. We are like the workers on a Gobelin tapestry.

The divine Artist sees and knows the marvels of art which we are producing, but we cannot see them or admire them until they are completed and taken from their frames.

When only twenty-one he wrote: "He who dies leaving his task unfinished is quite as advanced in the eyes of the supreme Justice as he who has the time to achieve it completely. The greatest men are those who have never drawn up in advance the plan of their lives, but have let themselves be led by the hand."

His arduous labors in lecturing, writing, studying and charity, made his life — so fragile and sickly — an amazingly full one. His spirit was sustained by the intimacies of family life, the reading of the Gospel every morning, and weekly Communion.

Five years after his marriage a daughter was born, who was christened Marie. "I am a father," he wrote to Foisset, "it is probably the greatest joy which one can experience here below." In his case the joy was not to be of long duration, for Marie was only a child of eight when her father died.

Was Ozanam a hindrance to the Catholic cause? This accusation was brought against him by Veuillot in the *Univers* in 1843, because he had in an address on "The Literary Obligations of Christians" recommended compassion for those who doubted, and urged his hearers not to pursue with insults those who denied the faith.

Surely Ozanam was no traitor. A refutation to this charge is to be found in Ozanam's own words, "I hold to Christian orthodoxy more than to life itself."

Writing in the *Correspondent* in 1850, he described the two schools of Catholics which were arrayed against each other in his day. The one school, to which Ozanam himself belonged, "had as its aim, to seek in the human heart all the secret cords which might draw it back to Catholicism, to go after souls that were lost, and to increase the number of Christians." He never permitted himself to insult any one — he who possessed rare gifts of irony, and abstained through charity from using them.

He considered that the special danger of his own school lay in a certain "softness or flabbiness, which would surrender something of the severity of dogma in a discussion, or the rights of the Church in the world of affairs." Lacordaire spoke of his tolerance as "a touching imitation of Our Lord, who never broke the bruised reed or quenched the smoking flax."

The other school, Ozanam accused of "presenting the truth to men, not in an aspect which would attract them, but in one which would repel them;

and of having no desire to convert unbelievers, but only to stir up the passions of believers."

Some days later in the *Univers* Veuillot charged Ozanam with "cowardly desertion," "soft complacency" and "denial." He immediately took up his pen to reply to Veuillot, and submitted what he wrote to Cornudet for his approval. His friend returned it to him with the words: "You are a Christian; forgive!"

Without hesitation Ozanam tore up his reply. Three months later, the Archbishop of Paris censured the *Univers*, and received a flood of congratulatory letters, but among them there was none from Ozanam. He never broke his silence.

ELIZABETH ARRIGHI LESEUR
[1866-1914]

HUSBANDS and wives who do not share the same mental and spiritual outlook often drift apart after the romantic glow of the early years of their married life disappears. If they are held together by an exceptionally deep affection, an intellectual tug-of-war will almost certainly persist until one gives in to the other. Difference in religious beliefs especially, if they are rooted in strong conviction, render conjugal harmony morally impossible.

One of the most dramatic episodes in recent spiritual history was the struggle that went on for many years between Elizabeth Leseur, a brilliant Frenchwoman, who was born in 1866 and died in 1914, and her husband Félix Leseur, who is still alive.

Elizabeth Arrighi was born in Paris of Catholic parents, her father being a lawyer, and she had the conventional bringing up of thousands of girls of her class in France in the last quarter of the nineteenth century. Her mother and sisters were good Catholics but not notably pious. She herself learned her catechism, made her first Communion, and received

Confirmation, without any signs of exceptional devotion.

In her twentieth year she became interested in Félix Leseur, a student of medicine. The fact that under the influence of his companions and professors he was losing his faith did not appear to be an insuperable obstacle to their becoming engaged three years later. He agreed to respect her faith, and they were married in 1889 in the Church of Saint-Germain-des-Près.

Madame Leseur was physically attractive, and with a manner full of distinction. Smiling and amiable, she was to the end attractive to children and young people. Gaiety was perhaps the predominant note of her character. Her fresh, frank laughter was familiar to all her friends. She was also a young woman of artistic and intellectual cultivation, deeply appreciative of the beautiful in painting, sculpture, music and literature. She read Latin easily, and conversed fluently in English and Russian. In her later years she mastered Italian.

Félix Leseur did not continue his studies in medicine, but became interested in foreign and colonial politics. During his student days he became a Modernist from his study of Strauss, Renan, Harnack and Loisy; and from this position he gradually drifted into atheism. His home became an anti-clerical centre, a favorite meeting-place for politicians, publicists, journalists, doctors, university men, scholars, men of letters, musicians, playwrights and artists. His wife, under the pressure of such surroundings, degenerated into a lax Catholic and almost gave up the practice of her religion. Her husband tried to convert her to an attitude of liberal Protestantism, hoping that this would be a half-way house to complete unbelief. He almost succeeded.

The turning-point in her life was the reading of Renan's *History of the Origins of Christianity*, on her husband's insistence. She could not but admit the glamour of his style, but what struck her most was the poverty and lameness of his arguments. Suddenly she sprang back, as if from the edge of an abyss. Realizing the immense value of what she was about to cast away, she devoted herself to a serious study of her religion. She began to collect a library of her own, consisting first of all of the Fathers, Doctors and the great mystics of the church. Above all she undertook a deep and prayerful study of the New Testament.

It was about this time, in her thirty-third year, that she began writing her *Spiritual Journal*, which has since proved so instructive and inspiring to thousands of readers. From it we learn how the spirit of detachment and the love of solitude took posses-

sion of her soul. Moreover, having strengthened
the foundations of her faith, she now responded to
her vocation to the intellectual apostolate.

The spiritual isolation consequent upon her conversion was relieved by the guidance of a wise father
in God who came into her life at this juncture. Acting as godmother at the baptism of the child of a
friend, she was introduced to a good Dominican friar,
whom she immediately chose as her spiritual director. After her death he told how greatly the penitent had edified the confessor, and testified that "she
was a true saint."

We find a summary of what she went through at
this time in a passage of her Journal, written October
19, 1911, wherein she gives a swift review of her
life : "When I look back, I see a childhood and
youth, even the beginnings of maturity, passed in
ignorance of and estrangement from God. I see
the first graces received while I was still young, not
sinking deep into me ; a path of indifference and
superficiality, with glimpses of fugitive light, swiftly
extinguished, perhaps by a mysterious divine will ;
the breaking of every link with God and the entire
forgetfulness of him in my heart ; then the slow,
silent action of Providence in me ; the wonderful
work of conversion, begun, controlled, completed by

God alone, outside all human influence or contact, sometimes by very means of that which should have lost me my faith. Then, when that divine task was done, the friend and guide of my soul was providentially put in my way. Then my reconciliation with God, the journey to Rome, and my consecration to Jesus Christ at the tomb of St. Peter." [1]

From this time on her supreme concern was the conversion of her husband. She resolved, however, never to give him the slightest hint of her dominant desire, never to give him annoyance by the practice of her religion or let it interfere with her wifely duties. Among her resolutions made in retreat was the following: "First, my duty to my dear husband: tenderness which was not even the merit of duty, constant care to be useful and gracious to him. Above all, to be extremely reserved concerning matters of faith, which are still veiled to him. If a quiet statement should sometimes be necessary, or if I can fruitfully show him a little of what is in my heart, that must at least be a rare event, performed in all gentleness. Let him see the fruit but not the sap, my life but not the faith that governs it, the light that is in me but not a word of him from whom it comes; let him see God without hearing his name. Only

---

[1] *A Wife's Story*, p. 161.

on those lines must I hope for the conversion and sanctity of the dear companion of my life, my beloved Félix."

It is plain from her *Journal* that it was simply through prayer and suffering that helped to bring about her husband's conversion, as well as that of the many other unbelievers who frequently came to her home. She suffered many trials and anxieties concerning those of her kindred whom she loved most, culminating in the death of her sister Juliette, which she considered the greatest grief of her life. Madame Leseur was a frequent invalid during the ten years before her own death, but endured her pains with patience and cheerfulness. She offered her life as a sacrificial victim for the conversion of her husband.

As Cardinal Amette, Archbishop of Paris, pointed out in a short introduction which he wrote for one of her books published after her death, she unawares drew a portrait of herself when in commenting on the Beatitude, *Blessed are the meek*, she wrote : "We have all met persons of this sort. They are rare, no doubt, but there flows from them such an intensity of inner life, such calm strength and such true beauty, that merely to come into contact with them soothes and comforts us. After all, this is only natural. Our outer life is the reproduction of our inner life, and the visible part of us reflects what is unseen ; we radiate our souls, so to say, and, when they are centres of light and warmth, other souls need only to be brought into contact with them in order to be warmed and enlightened. We give out, often unknown to ourselves, what we carry within us ; let us strive to increase daily this reserve store of faith and quiet charity."

Her *Journal* and most of her other spiritual writings have proven of real help to many in France and other countries. A possible exception might be the letter she wrote to her mother, which is published under the title, *A Call to the Interior Life*. To point out some of the short-comings of her aged mother seems to some readers to be lacking in Christian humility to say the least, even though she does it with the utmost delicacy.

She accepted boldly her vocation to the intellectual apostolate, which she exercised not only through personal conference, but through an active correspondence. She thus writes in her journal of this apostolate :

This is perhaps what God specially intends for me ; He has treated me like a "privileged child"; the word has been spoken to me and I know its truth ; He has arranged everything in me and about me to prepare me for that form of apostolate. In making known to me His intimate action in the soul, in placing me in the midst of negation and indifference and that impenetrable ignorance of divine things in which so many unfortunate people live, He has doubtless intended that I should understand the most widely differing states of mind, that I should show sympathy and turn towards blasphemy and doubt with special pity and love.

To be the good Samaritan to so many discontented hearts and uneasy minds and troubled consciences ; to feel delicate respect for souls and knowledge of them ; to approach them gently, to pour upon them healing oil or strengthening wine according to their weakness or the poignancy of their wound ; to show God only by letting Him shine forth from the soul where He lives ; to be all things to all men, and thus conquer souls to Christ is the apostle's task which I accept from Thee, my God, in spite of my unworthiness.[1]

[1] *A Wife's Story,* p. 116.

LUCIE FÉLIX-FAURE GOYAU
[1866-1913]

I HAVE been interested in the story of Lucie Félix-Faure Goyau.[1]   Her life is a good example of what an intelligent Catholic woman can accomplish in the literary apostolate.

Lucie Félix-Faure was born in 1866 in Amboise. She passed her childhood in Havre where her father was an export merchant, with extensive cosmopolitan interests.   She was his favorite child, and he spent most of his leisure time with her, and took her with him on his travels.   She was an omnivorous reader. In her thirteenth year she once ordered so many books from a Paris book-shop, that when the package arrived it bore the address: "Mademoiselle Lucie Faure, Bookseller, Havre."

When Lucie was seventeen, her father was elected to the Chamber of Deputies, and they moved to Paris.   Shortly afterwards he was made Secretary of State for the Colonies.   His home became a meeting-place for men of affairs, artists and men of letters. He visited most of the French possessions, and his

1 By J.-P. H. Heuzey, Paris, Perrin et Cie., 1916.

daughter always accompanied him. After a short term as Marine Minister, M. Félix-Faure was elected President of the French Republic in 1895. He held this office until his death four years later, when Lucie was thirty-three. As they had been bound together by the closest ties of intellectual and spiritual sympathy, the loss of her father caused her the keenest suffering of her life.

The library of the Élysee gave Lucie the opportunity to read everything of importance in contemporary literature. In her twenty-second year she had mastered Latin without the aid of a teacher, and became equally at home with the classics, the Fathers, and the mystics of the Middle Ages. She kept a journal in which she wrote down her impressions of what she read, as well as of what she saw on her travels. Thus she developed her literary vocation. Among the writers who gave her most to think about were Renan, Jules Simon, Fromentin, Balzac, Gauthier, Leconte de Lisle, Amiel, Emerson, Elizabeth Browning, and Cardinal Newman.

Naturally she had many opportunities of making a good marriage in the worldly sense. However, since her eighteenth year she had clung to the notion that marriage meant the absolute union of two hearts and two lives, and somehow the men whom her parents proposed to her as being promising both mate-

rially and morally did not seem to meet her require-
ments. When they said of one man that if she
would marry him she could always ride in a carriage,
she replied :

"I prefer to ride in an omnibus with a man whom
I love than in a carriage behind two horses with a
man whom I do not love."

On another occasion, when her parents thought
they had made a particularly good choice for her and
asked her why she had refused him, she answered :

"Because he does not like the Victory of Samo-
thrace."

It was not the sense of a vocation to the celibate
life that kept her from marrying. She had written
in her *Journal Intime :* "I do not at all think that
Christianity requires us to despise the beauty of the
human emotions ; we should rather recognize and
love the Divine in the natural order."

It was in 1897 that she finally met the man who
commanded her wholehearted respect and affection,
M. Georges Goyau, the Catholic publicist and histo-
rian. It was Newman that brought them together,
a beautiful recompense to her for writing so well of
him. She needed certain information for the book
she was writing, and a mutual friend introduced her
to M. Goyau as being the one who could best supply
it. That led to a frequent interchange of letters,

and M. Goyau soon became a zealous co-worker with Mlle. Félix-Faure in the League of the Children of France, which she had founded early in her sojourn at the Élysée. Her work on Newman appeared in 1900, and attracted wide attention. Three years later she became the wife of M. Goyau. Their home soon became one of the chief centers of Catholic intellectual life in Paris.

Madame Goyau's radiant personality drew to their fireside not only well-known Catholics of France, Germany, Italy and England — many of them ecclesiastics — but also the indifferent, unbelievers, scoffers at the faith. Tall and matronly, with supple, delicate hands, she welcomed all comers with her sympathetic smile and put them at their ease at once. Madame Duclaux, one of her intimate friends, said that her whole physiognomy expressed her soul, and drew this picture of her : "The nose, firm in outline and refined, spoke to me of her courage and loyalty of heart ; her kindly mouth, with regular, well-formed lips, revealed her qualities of purity and activity ; while in her restless eyelids, sometimes drawn down in sorrow over her charming eyes, I read the constant impulse of strong emotions."

Madame Alphonse Daudet has thus described her impression, when Madame Goyau received her at her country estate near Amboise : "The door opens and the mistress of the house appears. She looks big and handsome at the top of the steps, her features regular, hair already slightly grey, a tall figure, so like her father on the stairs of the Élysée. The habit of appearing in public has made her careful to be always dressed and ready to receive, and the kindly smile in the fine eyes gives a stamp of rather majestic grace to her whole person.

"We enter our hostess's *cabinet de travail*; the table is overladen with books of all sizes and shapes and every colour; and the walls are covered with pictures, engravings, portraits of saints of either sex, and Italian sovereigns. Lucie Goyau speaks to us with emotion of Saint Catherine of Genoa, whom she is just studying, and whom she reveals to us, so to speak. . ."

Her life at the Élysée had given her wide social experience, and her charm made her immensely popular. She came as near being "Princess Lucie," as a certain daughter of the White House did of being "Princess Alice." Yet how little beguiled Madame Goyau was by the fashionable life of the world may be judged from this allegory found among her private papers: "Let the approaches of the soul bloom with flowers, let them be embalmed with the divine perfume within, and let strangers who walk there experience the charm of it. We can always surrender the approaches, talk of art, literature, philosophy, or even of indifferent matters ; the perfume is there, it makes itself felt without expressing itself. Few discover the draw-bridge of the mysterious moat behind which is entrenched in all its splendour the crystal castle where burns the perpetual lamp in the presence of the Divinity, for that crystal castle is a sanctuary. The light of the lamp sends its rays out as far as the approaches ; the perfume of the sanctuary breathes out beyond the moat. Many come within the light and perceive the perfume. O my God, do they know the secret of the marvellous fire ?"

Her nature was essentially tender and mystical. Possessing to an unusual degree the power to influence her surroundings, she was a contemplative who did not fail to use every means to diffuse about her the inner secret of her soul.

God gave Lucie Goyau the grace to perform the moral miracle of living in the world with the recollectedness of a religious. Far from isolating her, the gift of genuine piety drew to her all who were bruised in heart. Even those who could not agree with her beliefs yielded to the spell of her presence. She made all worldly relationships the instruments of her apostolate ; and never permitted them to mar the effectiveness of her works of charity or the seriousness of her intellectual life. How she found the time for it is a mystery, but she managed to combine constant study and hours of contemplation with ceaseless beneficent activities. Besides the Fraternal League of the Children of France, which she founded to enable the children of the richer families to provide air, sunlight, vacations, for the children of the poor, she also established the *Syndicats Féminins* to make war on the sweating system, and the *Adelphie*, to provide means of livelihood for middle-aged women of the educated class who had suddenly become poor.

Her writings also gave vent to her remarkable store of energy ; but she looked upon them as a means not only of conversing but of converting. They give the impression of diversity, but in the main a sure instinct led her towards the subjects most suited to her special talent ; describing and commenting upon the feminine soul, especially in its Christian development. She was not a feminist in the vulgar sense ; but she had a noble and just conception of the place of women in social life. She realized that the time had passed when the ideal of the Roman matron, to stay at home and spin wool, could be imposed upon all women. She demanded for them everything which, while keeping them in their place and making their duties as women easier for them, might enlarge, enrich, embellish and deepen their lives.

Her work on Newman was somewhat youthfully ambitious, professing to treat as it did of "His Life and Works." She would not permit it to be reprinted. It appeared in 1900. She followed it in 1903 with *Méditerranée,* and with a book of verse called *La Vie Nuancée* in 1905. They were not noteworthy. Few women have shown a better understanding of women of the past than she did in her *Études d'Âme Féminine,* the first part of which dealt with women in the work of Dante. Her *Vie et Mort des Fées,* in 1910, was a brilliant essay in literary history. The best of her works was *Vers la Joie : Âmes Paiennes, Âmes Chretiennes,* the sixth edition of which was published in 1913. *Christianisme et Culture Féminine,* consisting of scattered papers and addresses delivered on various occasions, was published by her husband after her death.

She died on the Feast of Saint John Baptist in 1913 in her forty-seventh year. She had undergone two operations, the second complicated with pulmonary congestion, but in spite of months of pain, her joy was unfailing and she kept up her apostolate to the end.

The Abbé Bremond wrote, "It was not an agony, but a long silent canticle, the serene and sublime strophes of which we followed as she gazed on glories celestial." She had always insisted that "Christians should try to strip death of its sombreness." During the last days she was unconscious most of the time, but she always awoke to the Name of Jesus. An unbeliever who was present said :

"She responds to that name, as a soldier answers 'Present' at the call of battle."

In a prayer that she wrote "Before a Crucifix," which was sanctioned by Cardinal Mercier, there are two passages which, knowing her sincere humility, we may interpret as indicating that at the close of her live, she was not conscious of having grievously offended God, and that the faults of which she accused herself were rather neglected graces, lost opportunities of doing good :

"And it was not mortal sin ; no, my God . . . it was the neglect of graces, virtues that sought to expand and were held, crushed back by a personal impulse."

"In mine, O Jesus, I have crucified Thee. But love is stronger than death, and I hope to have escaped the true death of mortal sin."

As the Abbé Bremond remarks, Madame Goyau

was distinguished for her devotion to the light : "Responsive to the slightest hints of Providence, her baptismal name commended to her this magnificent devotion. Would that I had been able to tell her of an abbess of the sixteenth century whom I have recently encountered, *Luce de Lux,* with a name twice luminous. . . A soul of crystal, disdaining, forgetful of herself, unreservedly open to the light of heaven, and living only to take in and give forth this light — I do not think we can better describe Madame Goyau."

Undoubtedly this gives the key to her whole life. She rejoiced in believing that God made use of the hearts of his servants to give light to the world. The idea recurs constantly in her *Journal Intime* and other writings. "I know that I may give God," she wrote. Hence she was incorrigibly optimistic. She believed that here below good would always triumph over evil, because there were always saints ; and the efficacy of a single act of virtue, a single prayer, were boundless. She once said :

"When you shall have reformed your own soul, imagine that you have reformed the world. Every soul is a lever that may lift the world. No one can sanctify himself without elevating the whole human race."

Or again —

LUCIE FÉLIX-FAURE GOYAU

"When will people understand that one hour of intense interior life, enclosed within the limits of a narrow cell, contains something more decisive for humanity than the winning of this or that battle on the world's greatest battlefields?"

Father Léonce de Grandmaison, S.J., testified in an article on Madame Goyau in the *Constructive Quarterly* in 1914, that she exercised a remarkable apostolate of counsel, charity of the intellect, and expansion of Christian truth, because she never felt for the unbeliever or the impious the slightest repulsion or hatred, but only a lively and profound pity. They were to her the real poor, the most poor. To hundreds and thousands around her she applied the words of the old Hebrew prophet, as suffering from the famine of the words of Jehovah. Father Grandmaison goes on to say: "In recalling these matters we are, of course, obliged to maintain a considerable reserve; it is, nevertheless, necessary to insist upon this feature on pain of leaving in shadow that which was most notable in this distinguished woman. She always had the feeling, and a sort of intuition, of the spiritual needs of souls. Very accessible, generous, far removed from all zealot bitterness, she was all the more persuasive when speaking of the benefits, the beauty, the security, of Catholic convictions. Not only tempted or tepid men, but even priests;

not only her co-religionists, but Protestants and Israelites in numbers were thus touched, convinced, converted."

I have purposely quoted the testimony of such masters of the spiritual life as Father Grandmaison and the Abbé Bremond, lest it be thought that my account of her is unduly enthusiastic.

I will end by letting Madame Goyau speak for herself. In a passage of rare beauty, she unconsciously gives expression to what she wished her life to be, an ascent in the light towards greater light:

"The human personality will never be annihilated: it has the promise of eternity. But it may be overwhelmed, invaded, submerged, just as a fragment of crystal is overwhelmed, invaded, submerged by the light. It disappears, but it does not cease to exist; it is the glory of its purity to lose itself and let the pure and glorious light pass through it without hindrance.

"All its transparency will not annihilate it; it is given up to the light which penetrates without breaking it. Now it must be entirely given up if it is to be true to its mission; should it refuse anything to the light, it would then be wishing itself to carry darkness and would be fancying itself adding to its own existence by this love of the darkness, which would be the inordinate love of its own personality. To carry darkness, it must be smoke-begrimed, dusty, obscured, and must delight in its own smoke, dust, and obscurity ; it would believe itself happy in carrying a shadow in the sunlight. Thus the darkened and blinded soul believes itself to be enjoying what it refuses to God. Souls are like crystal : their true mission and their true joy is transparency to the Light which is Love."

THREE APOSTLES OF CATHOLIC ACTION

What is Catholic Action?

A GOOD Catholic layman will not be content to go through life letting the Church do things for him and to him. He will feel that he ought also to do something for the Church. Those who love Our Lord will try to walk in His steps and strive daily to become more like Him. He said himself that the Son of Man came not to be ministered unto but to minister, and to give His life a redemption for many; therefore those who love Him will not be satisfied in letting the Church minister to them, but will also want to minister to the Church.

The Church is in the world not merely to save us, but through our faith and charity to save others as well. This applies not only to priests but to the laity. The zealous man will aim so to practice his religion and fulfil the obligations of his state in life that the Catholic Church may be brought within the range of practical possibilities for all men of good will.

Furthermore the Catholic layman will wish to perform whatever spiritual work he may undertake under the direction of and in coöperation with the duly constituted authorities of the Church. This suggests what is meant by Catholic Action. It is the participation and collaboration of the laity with the apostolic hierarchy of the Church, outside of and above political parties, for the establishment of the universal kingdom of Jesus Christ.

If a layman should act independently and take up any work he thought needed to be done, he might enter upon a task for which he was not fitted or which he could not finish, or he might interfere with a work already being done by others. It is better to act under orders from above. A private soldier is more useful in time of war, when he fulfils the orders of his commanding officers than when he makes individual attacks on his own initiative. The Church militant is always at war.

The Holy Father, Pius XI, has said on many occasions that Catholic Action is as dear to him as the pupil of his eye. It has been called "the supernatural patriotism of men in the service of Christ, and the devoted resolve to work for the spread and triumph of His kingdom on earth."[1]

Catholic Action fulfils one of the desires most dear

---

[1] Father Bernard Delany, O.P., *The Clergy Review*, April, 1933, p. 304.

to the heart of God, namely, union — the intimate union of the laity with the hierarchy, and of the hierarchy itself. It combines all the conditions of a true apostolate of the Church, to which victories of temporal and spiritual regeneration are promised. Thus Catholics and their leaders, instead of confessing themselves powerless and disarmed, form an indestructible *bloc*, after the manner of the early Christians in Jerusalem, who had but one heart and one soul. The organization of the Catholic laity, participating in the hierarchical apostolate, is a turning-point in the history of the Church, which will always remember Pius XI as essentially the Pope of Catholic Action.

There have been few more critical periods in the history of the Church than the sixty years in Italy that followed the destruction of the Temporal Power of the Papacy in 1870. The success of the *Risorgimiento*, coupled with the physical defeat of Pius IX, ushered in the liberal era in Italy, when religion was declared to be but the private concern of the individual. It was the professed aim of those in control of United Italy that ultimately all life would be freed from what they called the thraldom of religion. This triumph of materialism was to be brought about first of all by the secularizing of education. The Pope forbade Catholics to vote in the national elections, and thereby to countenance this new program. Consequently it required moral courage for an Italian layman to be a good Catholic in those days. The State and the Church were in conflict, and he had to decide which had the higher claim on his allegiance. Many secular and economic advantages would be his if he decided in favor of the State.

Three laymen stand out as leaders of Catholic Action during these difficult years : Count Paganuzzi, Professor Toniolo, and Doctor Necchi—a lawyer, a professor of economics, and a physician. They concerned themselves respectively with three successive phases in the defensive movement which has resulted in the reversal of conditions with which we are familiar today. Paganuzzi was occupied primarily with the Roman question and the defense of the Papacy. Professor Toniolo worked out a Catholic solution to the social and economic problems, the pressure of which was alienating the working classes from the Church. Ludovico Necchi, in addition to his professional work, coöperated in the founding of the Catholic University of the Sacred Heart at Milan.

GIAMBATTISTA PAGANUZZI
[1830-1910]

THIS unyielding defender of the papal claims was a Venetian lawyer. He was a man of strong personal magnetism, incorruptible integrity, and warm affections. He put his legal services at the disposal of the Church and the poor, and refused to take from them any fee. His mildness towards individuals was joined with the ardor of an absolute intransigent in the field of doctrine. This indefatigable worker found his recreation in study, because he was convinced that he could be of little help to the Catholic cause without knowledge.

In a time of frightened and lukewarm faith, Count Paganuzzi was the champion of the Christian, Catholic, papal idea. For that idea he lived and suffered, wrestled like a lion, sacrificed himself, his soul full of poetry and joy. He cherished the dream of introducing and preserving sane principles in the social life of Italy; and in the pursuit of his task he ignored both praises and insults.[1]

[1] *Venezia nella via contemporanea e nella storia*, by Gine Bertolini, p. 356.

In 1889, Italian Catholics were not as yet conscious of the necessity of becoming organized nationally; and therefore Paganuzzi gladly assumed the leadership in the works of the Catholic Congresses (*L'Opera dei Congressi Cattolici*). Unity of opinion or of action here and there was not enough; there must be solidarity of action by a national movement. To him the end of Catholic Action was nothing less than the Kingship of Jesus Christ, the propagation of the faith, the victory of the Church, the defence and triumph of the Papacy, the education and salvation of souls; all the other things were only means to these ends. Catholic Action to Paganuzzi was a true apostolate, with the aim of arousing the laity by the appeal of Saint Ignatius : *Ite, incendite, inflammate.*

Such a national organization of Catholics, according to Paganuzzi, must have certain characteristics. First of all, it should be eminently religious. It should be inspired by a Christian and Catholic spirit, even in its economic and social manifestations. It was the religious sentiment and principle he insisted which moved, vivified and warmed everything in Italy ; outside the faith there remained only what was sick, moribund and cadaverous. Secondly, it should result in the profound transformation of the individual according to the laws of Christian perfection. Without this it would be vain to hope for the improvement and restoration of society. Thirdly, with such transformation of the individual and society, there would be some assurance that the promoters of the Catholic movement in Italy and their friends and followers would not belong to that lamentable class which professed the Catholic religion but did not practise it.

Paganuzzi realized the danger of a movement which was not under the direction of the ecclesiastical authorities. He often had to hold in check aggressive individuals who insisted on exercising the franchise, in spite of the papal veto. It was due to him that the work of the Congresses remained subject to the hierarchy. He said repeatedly that whatever good results the Congresses of Catholic laymen might be able to accomplish, was not due to the laity, their words or their weak authority ; it was rather due to the authority of their pastors, and principally of their bishops, who spoke in their own name and in that of the Holy Father. The bishops, he said, graciously presided in their assemblies and spoke in them ; and it was their inspired and venerated words, penetrating the secrets of all hearts, that gave to their works of Catholic Action an authority which they would not otherwise have had.

Undoubtedly Count Paganuzzi had the defects of

his qualities. Strongly preoccupied as he was with the Roman question, he did not perceive perhaps the inevitability and the value of other currents of thought. The need of the Christian apostolate, as the informative principle of Catholic Action, was so vivid in his mind that he could not for an instant see things from any other standpoint. The events proved that he was largely right.

But at the time, it seemed as if the younger men were being alienated from the Congress Movement and joining the movement led by Dom Romulo Murri. The conflict between Murri and Paganuzzi was not so much regarding the practical means of organizing and assisting the proletariat, but the spirit which should inform their social activity. Murri wished it to be independent of the Church; Paganuzzi believed it should be under the guidance of her authority. Although Pope Leo XIII repeatedly condemned every tendency towards making the movement irreligious and autonomous, he nevertheless accepted the resignation of Paganuzzi as President of the Works of the Congresses.

On this occasion Pope Leo XIII manifested his gratitude to Paganuzzi by creating him Knight of the Grand Cross of the Order of Saint Gregory the Great. Already in 1874, Pius IX had made him a Knight of Saint Gregory the Great; and Leo XIII in 1882 had made him Honorary Chamberlain of the Cloak and Sword. Finally in 1896 he was made Roman Count. Pius X, who as Patriarch of Venice had been devoted to Paganuzzi, always entertained for him a lively esteem which later ripened in friendship.

In 1908, Paganuzzi and his daughter, who for years had been his most intimate companion, made the ascent of Monte Baldo. While he rested in the mountain refuge, his daughter collected a bunch of *edelweiss* and brought it to her father. Fixing upon her his luminous eyes, he said :

"We will send the most beautiful of them to the Holy Father."

"But, father," she asked, "do you want to send flowers to the Pope ?"

"Yes," he replied, "because up here we are able to send him the most beautiful flowers in the world."

A few days later these modest *edelweiss* arrived at the Vatican and Pius X was deeply touched by the gift. Did they not represent a beautiful life dedicated uniquely to the Vicar of Christ ?

GIUSEPPE TONIOLO
[1845-1918]

IN THE last quarter of the nineteenth century, when
the Roman question was the chief concern of Italian
Catholics like Paganuzzi, social problems did not receive the attention that Catholics gave them north of
the Alps. In Germany, Monsignor Ketteler had
met the propaganda of Lassalle by raising the ban-
ner of Catholic Social Reform. In Italy, before the
Encyclical *Rerum Novarum* had cleared the air,
Catholic Social Reformers found it difficult to enter
the *Opera dei Congressi*, against the stubborn resistance of its President, Count Paganuzzi.

It had been due to the mistaken political policy of
Metternich that previous to 1870 the fortunes of the
Church were linked with the continuance in power of
the various royal houses of Italy. Hence the *Risorgimiento* took on an anti-clerical aspect. It was
assumed that the clergy like the kings would sink
into oblivion. The result was that in the liberal era
which followed 1870, a great gulf was fixed between
the Church and society. Art, science, politics and
economics developed on non-Christian lines. Two

serious conflicts marked this period of Italian history ; the conflict between Church and State, and that between faith and reason. In consequence the educated classes became religiously indifferent ; and anti-clerical socialism spread rapidly among the working classes.

That the Catholic Church was finally recognized to be on the side of the working classes in their struggle against exploitation by the liberal *bourgeoisie*, was due, under God, to Pope Leo XIII and the teachings of Giuseppe Toniolo.

Born in Treviso on the Feast of Saint Thomas Aquinas in 1845, he was educated at the University of Padua, and early developed a strong preference for sociology. When only twenty-three he became assistant lecturer in economics at Padua ; and in 1878 was nominated to the chair of political economy in the University of Pisa.

His position was difficult because of his outspoken clerical sympathies. One of his superiors, Professor Luzzatti, a Jew, tried to put his young protégé on his guard by warning him :

"You go too often to Mass and confession, Toniolo."

He did not heed the warning. Later on, in 1898, when the Liberal government was enforcing its repressive measures against socialism, Professor Toniolo was secretly denounced to the government as a "clerical socialist," and was in danger of losing his professorship.

These two incidents throw light on his economic philosophy. He ever remained a loyal Catholic, but his wide social sympathies made him incline to the side of the workers in their conflict with a heartless, irreligious capitalism.

The Catholic Church has always defended the right of private property, but insists that it be distributed so that every one may possess something. She has championed the cause of the poor, and sought to raise their standards of living so that they will be equal to those of the privileged classes. The revolt against the authority of the Church in the sixteenth century destroyed the control of the social-temporal order by the Church and resulted in the bourgeois capitalist industrial order. The rise of capitalism led to the growth of modern industrialism; industrialism created the proletariat; and the proletariat is now agitating for collectivism, whereby all will be dragged down to the level of the wage-earners.

The fundamental issue between Catholicism and communism is whether human beings shall be raised to the dignity of free men or degraded to the ignominy of bread-tickets and slavery. There is little difference between wage-slavery under an unregulated plutocracy and slavery under a communist State. Leo XIII, in his *Rerum Novarum*, which was completely in accord with the economic theories of Professor Toniolo, and Pius XI, in his *Quadragesimo Anno*, have been voices crying out in the wilderness of the modern world calling upon men to repent of the evils of plutocracy and communism, and return to the principles of true Christian democracy.

In the liberal era which prevailed in Italy during the closing years of the nineteenth century, the Church found that a merely negative criticism of liberalism was not enough. If she was to gain popular support in her opposition to liberalism, especially among the working classes who were rapidly becoming socialistic, she must make it clear that she had a constructive economic policy. The man who at this juncture came forward as the trusted spokesman of Leo XIII, and the leader of the Christian Democratic Movement in Italy, was Giuseppe Toniolo.

In July, 1897, he expressed his views in an article on "The Christian Conception of Democracy" in the *Rivista Internazionale de Scienze Economiche e Sociali*, of which he was editor. The proofs were in the possession of Leo XIII for a week before they were finally sent to the printer, and the Holy Father gave the article his unqualified approval. When it appeared, it attracted wide attention among students of social problems on both sides of the Alps.

Toniolo maintained that the special conception of democracy which the Catholic Church had given to the world was that the learned, the well-to-do and the powerful should lift up those who were beneath them in the social scale. The well-being of the masses must therefore be the chief aim of any social order worthy of the Christian name. The prevailing conception of society was based on the assumption that the privileged few had the right to exploit the unprivileged masses. This assumption was the outgrowth of the materialistic capitalism which originated in the sixteenth century and has since dominated the countries which were chiefly affected by the Reformation — Germany, the Netherlands, Scandinavia, Great Britain and America. They have set the pace for the economic and industrial developments of the last four centuries. The weakness of the Catholic Church in those countries has until recently prevented her from setting forth her social and industrial program. In consequence an uncontrolled and ruthless capitalism has driven the working classes to socialism and communism.

Toniolo defined democracy as "that condition of society in which the legal and economic factors, in their complete hierarchical development, are so harmonized that each in due proportion contributes its share towards the well-being of the entire community and in such a manner that the greatest benefit of all is reaped by those classes situated at the bottom of the social structure."

Borrowing his fundamental principles from the Thomistic philosophy, Toniolo was firmly convinced that the State was made for man, and not man for the State. He became the foremost representative in his day of the Christian school of sociology. "This school," he wrote, "is mainly distinguished by its subordination of economics to Christian ethics, inasmuch as it recognizes the scientific and practical legitimacy of the law of utility only when this does not run counter to the higher law of duty ; when, in fact, it leads to the moral goal of individual, civil and religious perfection."

The ultimate unit of any constructive schemes of social reform, in Toniolo's opinion, must be the Christian family, which alone can keep aflame and pass on to future generations the torch of Christian faith. Such families contain the dynamic for the moral regeneration of society.[1]

In spite of his deeply religious nature, Toniolo never felt the call to the priesthood or the religious

[1] The above quotations are from the Catholic Truth Society's publication, *Giuseppe Toniolo*, by Reverend H. L. Hughes, to whom I owe all my facts about Toniolo.

life ; he believed it was his mission to remain in the world and carry on the lay apostolate of Catholic Action. This he tried to do through his teaching and writing, but also as husband and father.

In his thirty-third year, realizing the need of a sympathetic companion to help him in his work, he married Maria Schiratti of Venice. She was a remarkable woman, and became in truth the "angel in the house" ; their union was an ideal intellectual and spiritual relationship. She outlived him, and died in their old home in Pisa in 1929.

This kindly professor and leader in Catholic social reform looked upon parenthood as definitely a religious vocation, and his children as "talents" committed to his trust, which might be made to yield an hundred-fold. He gave the most loving attention to the training of their minds and characters ; and on holidays took them for long walks in the country, explaining to them the secrets of nature. He often rocked his infants to sleep. Every morning before breakfast he read to his wife and children a page of the Gospels ; and at night, after leading them in family prayers, gave them his paternal blessing.

To his students in the University he never seemed an austere man of science, but rather a kind father and friend. He often invited a group of them to spend the evening at his home, where they could dis-

cuss points in his lectures which they had not understood. He encouraged them to express their own
opinions freely, and knew how to suggest a simple
solution to their difficulties. He never probed their
consciences ; but they often told him their moral per-
plexities, and sought his advice.

He died in 1918, just as the news came in that
Germany and Austria had requested an armistice.
With prophetic insight he said sadly, "We are not
yet ready for peace !" They were almost his last
words. When the end had come, his wife, children
and grandchildren, following an old family custom,
knelt round the bed and sang the *Te Deum*.

It was a fitting end to a life, which — in the words
of his old friend and colleague, the Jewish Professor
Luzzatti — had indeed been the life of a "lay saint."

LUDOVICO NECCHI
[1876-1930]

EARLY in his boyhood, Vico, as he was called by his friends, gave evidence of moral courage. One day in school, his teacher — an unfrocked priest — stood beside Vico's desk, towering over the boy, and bellowed out in contemptuous tones:

"You little fool, you don't really believe in the temporal power of the Pope, do you?"

"Yes, sir," he replied promptly, and went on with his studies.

One of his most intimate boyhood friends was Agostino Gemelli; and it is impossible to tell the story of either without bringing in the other. They both intended to study medicine and entered the University of Pavia at the same time.

Gemelli, impelled by the anti-clerical trend of university life in those days, became the leader of the socialist students and editor of their magazine, entitled *The People*. Necchi, having been chosen president of the Saint Severinus Boethius Catholic Club, instituted the practice of inviting non-Catholic students to attend the meetings of the club. Heated discussions often went on till a late hour, with Gemelli as the chief opponent of the Catholic position.

Necchi had already gained notoriety as an advocate of Christian democracy, dividing his time between his studies and the headquarters of the Christian Democratic Movement in Milan. On Sunday mornings he was accustomed to go out on speech-making tours among the agricultural laborers of the surrounding districts. As it was necessary to start very early, he often fasted till one o'clock in order to be able to receive Holy Communion.

After taking his medical degree, he was assigned for the time of his military service to the army hospital of Saint Ambrose in Milan. Doctor Gemelli was assigned to the same hospital and the beds of the two old friends were next each other. They continued in the hospital the discussions which they had begun at Pavia. Owing to their position as doctors, they were given a small room in which to perform their scientific experiments. Their talk often turned on the fundamental problems of life and religion. In the midst of a heated argument, Necchi suggested one day to his friend that he say daily the following prayer:

"O God, if you exist, make yourself known to me."

Gemelli noticed that Necchi slipped out of his bed

early every morning to attend Mass in the nuns' chapel attached to the hospital. He did not know that Vico received Holy Communion daily and prayed for the grace of conversion for his friend.

One evening Gemelli said to him : "Listen, Vico, wake me early when you get up tomorrow morning. I am curious to see what you go and do. I should like to come with you."

"Come, by all means," answered his friend.

When they entered the chapel, the sceptical Gemelli remained standing with folded arms throughout the Mass. When they went out together, he seemed as cold and indifferent as before. They continued their discussions.

Then came Good Friday in the year 1903. Necchi was astonished to hear his friend say to him :

"Necchi, come with me to church !"

On entering the Basilica of Saint Ambrose, Gemelli fell on his knees and buried his face in his hands. After a few moments of prayer, he stood up and said :

"Take me to see a priest !"

Necchi took him first for confession to Father Pini, and afterwards to his old friend and spiritual director, Father Mattiusi, who later succeeded Cardinal Billot as Professor of Theology in the Gregorian University in Rome.

Gemelli was not a man of half measures. He at once decided to sacrifice his promising career in medicine and consecrate his whole life to the service of God. In spite of its involving a painful break with his family, he entered a Franciscan monastery. There followed sarcastic comments in the liberal press about the socialist doctor who had become a friar.

Necchi was married in his thirtieth year to Donna Vittoria della Silva De Rido Castiglioni and his family life was supremely happy. He allowed nothing to come before his family and the interests of his children.

"Oh, Vico Necchi's children!" to quote Father Gemelli, "for them he was ready to sacrifice his studies and all outside attractions. He considered the education of his child such an important duty that he overlooked nothing, from their material welfare in infancy to their moral well-being during their youth. He was able to tell his sons later that he had never left them in contact with persons, surroundings or other things with which he was not fully conversant."

Today Father Gemelli is the Rector of the Catholic University of the Sacred Heart, whose magnificent new buildings occupy the site of the old military hospital of Saint Ambrose, which was the scene of his conversion. To these two friends, Gemelli and Necchi, are chiefly due, under God, the rapid growth of the University till it has become one of the most flourishing centers of learning in Italy. At the time of his death, Necchi held the chair of biology; and he brought to it the wide philosophical training which enabled him to deal with the perplexing biological problems of the day.

When the opportunity was offered to purchase the ex-Cistercian monastery which had become the military hospital of Saint Ambrose, Father Gemelli exclaimed enthusiastically to Doctor Necchi:

"Just fancy, Necchi, if we were to go to St. Ambrose! We could build a chapel for ourselves right up at the top. You remember where?" He pointed upward to the chapel where he had first gone to Mass with Necchi.

"Let us promise," said the Friar, "to build a great statue of the Sacred Heart in the Piazza S. Ambrogio, if we are able to purchase the military hospital."

"Yes," answered Necchi, "let us make this promise."

Eleven million lire were contributed by the generous Catholics of Italy, and the site was purchased. On the façade of the new building facing the Piazza is an imposing statue of Christ the King holding in his hands close to his flaming heart the globe of the world.

The visitor to the new building of this University — the last word in educational efficiency — will realize how symbolical is this statue of the invincible faith in Christ which enabled these two friends to build so wisely for the future of Catholic education in Italy.

He will not forget the bas-relief of the head of Ludovico Necchi, lying peacefully on a pillow in the sleep of death, and the epitaph which was dictated by Father Gemelli in a moment of tense emotion :

MAY THE RARE BEAUTY OF THE SOUL OF
DOCTOR COMMENDATORE LUDOVICO NECCHI VILLA,
A FRANCISCAN TERTIARY,
MEMBER OF THE FOUNDATION AND ADMINISTRATIVE
COMMITTEES
OF THE CATHOLIC UNIVERSITY OF THE SACRED HEART,
FAITHFUL TO OUR LORD JESUS CHRIST,
FROM THE DAYBREAK TO THE SUNSET OF HIS LIFE,
INFLEXIBLE IN VIRTUE, YET GENTLE IN FIRMNESS,
HIGH-MINDED IN AFFECTION, STUDY AND WORK,
SHINE FOR EVER IN THE GLORY OF GOD, OUR FATHER.

*   *   *   *   *

It was at the conclusion of Doctor Necchi's military service that he faced the problem of his vocation.

[334]

He was uncertain whether he was called to the priesthood or the responsibilities of family life. To gain divine guidance he made a six days' retreat in a house of the Jesuit Fathers at Satirana. Among the notes made during the retreat was found this record of his decision :

As regards my state in life, it seems clear to me that it is God's will that I should remain in the world, as a school for my spiritual improvement. I trust that this decision has been in no wise influenced by any pandering to sensuality or human considerations. I decide to follow my vocation for study and research work, viewing this in the light of a duty, as a means of giving glory to God, leaving the results entirely in His hands.

In his work as physician he exercised a deep moral and spiritual influence over patients while trying to discover the physical and mental causes of their ailments. He had studied neuropathology in Germany, specializing in the psycho-neuroses. For ten years he devoted much time to the home for abnormal children established by Father Gemelli in Milan, bestowing the most meticulous care on each child.

The secret of his success as a neuropathologist lay not only in his adequate preparation, but in a warm personal sympathy for his patients springing from the fact that he was a fellow-sufferer.

He once said to Father Gemelli : "In order to

acquire that degree of self-denial necessary to cure these diseases—a spirit of self-sacrifice which no motive of mere financial gain or of scientific interest is powerful enough to create—in order to enter into the patient's mind, to understand by intuition what he tries to express in halting language and so spare him the ordeal of making a long and painful confession, one must have undergone these torments oneself. *And I have suffered them.*"

Father Gemelli goes on to tell us some things of Doctor Necchi's methods of psychiatric treatment, which clearly reveal the manner of man he was:

He told me something of the sufferings he had undergone, and at last I understood what had previously been a mystery to me, namely why at a certain period in his life I had been obliged to insist for a long time in order to induce him to receive Holy Communion, when he had such a great devotion to the Eucharist and had been accustomed to daily Communion from childhood. I remembered how I had broken down his resistance only as a last resort by making use of my priestly authority. For it is well to bear in mind that our friendship was of such a nature that if in the external affairs of this world I considered him my senior, in virtue of my priestly dignity and the consecration of my life to God's service, he looked up to me as his leader and guide. Whenever I spoke as a priest, he always accepted my decision without discussion. So it came about that he eventually accepted this work gladly, since it gave him the opportunity of showing his gratitude to God for freeing him from the torments of a life of morbid fears and scruples, from a state of health which would have been diagnosed by nine doctors out of ten as neurasthenia, but in which none the less lay at stake the well-being of his whole moral, intellectual and religious life.

In treating these cases Ludovico Necchi adopted those remedies which his own personal experience had taught him were most effective. Naturally — and in this he showed his knowledge of human nature — he did not place before his patients straight away a vision of the supernatural as a remedy for their ailments, supplying them with a general formula which each patient would have had to swallow almost like a medicine. Such a method would have been no good at all. Instead, to each patient he proposed the same remedy in a different manner. Once having learnt the sick man's history, his mistakes, the points where he had gone wrong, and his distorted and twisted notions of the meaning and value of life, he then proceeded to show the patient how to build up his life again, to check his inordinate cravings for human affection, regulate his desires and realize his highest aspirations. In a word he attempted to make the patient himself build his own supernatural life by trying to get him to view things from a supernatural angle. The main remedy used, then, by Doctor Necchi was to increase the confidence of his patients in the providence of God. This was the remedy he had found most effective in his own case. He had had his own doubts, uncertainties, torments, and anxieties, or, more exactly, had passed through a period not so much of spiritual crisis as of spiritual illness . . . and perhaps God had allowed this so that Necchi should possess that profound sense of pity and compassion so necessary in order to have the patience to cure people afflicted with maladies of this nature. The time and manner of his own return to normal conditions of health inclines one to accept this supposition. He repeatedly affirmed in after years that he was completely cured, and that a sense of peace had come back to him owing to an ever-increasing conviction that God guides our footsteps, even in the smallest matters, along mysterious paths, in order to bring about the fulfilment of his own designs.[1]

[1] *Ludovico Necchi,* by Monsignor Olgiati, p. 45. English translation by Reverend Henry L. Hughes, B.A., D.Litt., Catholic Truth Society.